P9-CLS-157

Andrew Matheson

LEICA
Rangefinder Practice
M6 TO M1

HOVE FOTO BOOKS

FIRST ENGLISH EDITION September 1986

Translated and revised for English Edition by the author from original German Edition.

ISBN 0 906447-37-2

Published by
HOVE FOTO BOOKS
34 Church Road
Hove, East Sussex
BN3 2GJ
United Kingdom

U.K. Trade Distribution
Fountain Press Ltd
45 The Broaday
Tolworth, Surrey
KT6 7DW

U.S.A. Distribution
Seven Hills Books
49 Central Avenue
Suite 300
Cincinnati
Ohio 45202

Typeset by Arachne Marketing Services
Printed in Great Britain by Purnell Book Productions Ltd
A member of BPCC plc

CONTENTS

ACKNOWLEDGEMENTS

The Author and Publisher would like to thank Ernst Leitz Wetzlar GmbH for their technical assistance in helping to make this book as accurate as possible and for their permission to use their registered Trade Marks. The following Trade Marks occur in the book:—

Leica®
LEICA®
ELMAR®
ELMARIT®
SUMMARON®
SUMMICRON®
SUMMILUX®
NOCTILUX®
TELYT®
LEICAVIT®
TELEVIT®
VISOFLEX®
PRADOVIT®
REPROVIT®
FOCOMAT®

The Leica: A Living Legend

Without doubt the Leica is photography's most famous camera. Its unique and almost continuous production history extends for over sixty years — during which it underwent just one major design change. In appearance the lastest Leica M6 hardly differs from the Leica M3 introduced in the early 1950s.

At best, the Volkswagen 'Beetle' motor car offers the nearest comparable industrial product tradition — but that kept its individual appearance for only half as long as the Leica. (Today's Volkswagens look as anonymous as any other medium-size car.)

How the Leica came into being has been described a thousand times over, so here is just a brief summary: engaged around 1912 in designing a motion picture camera, engineer Oskar Barnack at Leitz also built a small camera body for test exposure on 35 mm cine film. The results encouraged Barnack to follow up an earlier photographic ambition of producing big prints by enlarging small negatives — especially when he doubled the 18 × 24 mm cine frame area to 24 × 36 mm. Over the next few years Barnack used his home-made camera for much private photography and in 1923 developed it to a production camera for Leitz, who marketed it as the LEICA in 1925. Initially the LEICA attracted little attention (the total production of the first three years was under six thousand cameras) but in the early 1930s it became unexpectedly popular, creating a whole technique of miniature camera photography.

The causes lay in novel factors that we take for granted today.

Firstly, for its time the LEICA was decidedly a precision camera — at a period when camera contructuion involved scant precision engineering. It was therefore able to exploit the scope of the 24 × 36 mm image frame. (There had been earlier 35 mm cameras — but with serious quality and design shortcomings. On the other hand even medium-price cameras of today easily meet and surpass the primitive quality levels of those days.

Secondly, this small and handy camera encouraged a candid picture taking approach, matching a more casual life style that was just becoming fashionable. The miniature camera, almost for the first time, captured slices of life, not just posed set-ups. Even Barnack's own feature records of the previous decade reflected this.

LEICA pictures by amateur and later professional photographers, published in books and periodicals, widely publicised the range of this camera.

Thirdly, to realise this scope photographers needed — and were soon offered — substantial improvements in image quality with finer grain and high film resolution as well as better lens performance.

Finally there was the evolution of an equipment system. With lenses of alternative focal lengths the photographer could control image scale and angle of view. The coupled rangefinder, built in since 1932, established the rangefinder LEICA. A growing number of accessories — close-up aids, single-exposure housings and film holders, reflex attachments, focusing slides, turrets, micro-attachments, copying stands and more — within very few years evolved into a versatile and incredibly extensive modular equipment system. Thus the Leica was the first true camera system which not only brought into being the idea of a universal camera for special applications but also advanced far into scientific, technical, industrial and other fields of applied photography.

What counted was the extended system. Interchangeable lenses and quite a few other camera accessories had been known before. New was the modular approach: instead of different cameras for different applications the LEICA uses the most suitable special accessory or unit for a given application. Some of these accessories eventually got installed in the camera body itself — for instance motors, exposure metering and control systems, or reflex housings. The latter indeed turned the rangefinder miniature into today's SLR.

This almost graphic image depends on pattern — the black-and-white rendering provides the perfect treatment. *Photo: Hans Weinberger.*

Sixty years of Leica tradition

This book deals with the rangefinder Leica which started to make the name known from 1925 onwards. The latest version is the 1984 model M6 with built-in exposure metering. We shall deal with it in detail in the following chapters. The built-in combined viewfinder and rangefinder with bright-line frames and the bayonet lens mount were established back in 1953 with the model M3. That initiated the present M-series design. During the thirty-odd years since then, Leitz have produced some sixteen variations of the LEICA M type — or over twenty if one counts black and chrome models separately. (There was even a gold-plated Leica — see the LEICA HISTORY chapter.) They differ in details of the finder, in motor drive coupling, frame counter, selftimer and exposure metering. Yet they look remarkably alike — a unique continuity among camera brands.

Until 1960 there was a LEICA series with a screw lens mount and a body design largely derived from the first 1925 Leica. Lens interchangeability arrived in 1930 and the coupled rangefinder soon after. There are more than thirty versions of these LEICAS from the model I to the IIIg (with and without rangefinder, slow shutter speeds, eventually flash synch etc), but these again maintained a fairly uniform design.

In terms of production numbers the LEICA lags well behind modern mass-produced cameras, though the classical Leica did manage to run to some 1.3 million units. Just under 800,000 of them were screw-mount LEICAS (including the first 60,000 with non-interchangeable lenses); the M-range accounted for around half a million. One aspect of the development of this camera is that early models soon became collectors' items. One factor favouring that was that certain models or variations appeared in very small runs, including special (and sometimes gold-plated) jubilee editions. Other specially engraved models — for instance supplied at various times to German, British, American, Swedish and other armed forces — also tend to have appreciable rarity value. However, this has little to do with photography.

Nominally related to the Leica (and in part made in the same factory) are the Leicaflex single-lens reflexes from 1965 onwards, later becoming the LEICA R models (R3, R4, R4s). Not counting alternative black/chrome versions, this SLR range in the past twenty years also managed to reach around ten variants — even if model names changed more slowly. They are cameras of supreme precision engineering but hardly of revolutionary design. The SLR had other pioneers.

Where the rangefinder scores

Today the 35 mm SLR however is largely the successor of the rangefinder miniature. Its manufacturers currently produce some six million units a year world-wide, or about a thousand times as many as 35 mm precision rangefinder cameras. Despite the advantages of the SLR — direct screen focusing and accurate viewing with all focal lengths, especially zooms and in the macro range — the LEICA has survived, though it is virtually the only rangefinder system camera to have done so. For it still has the special merits with which in its day it established 35 mm photography as a new picture taking approach. And in some respects the reflex has lost something of this intimate pictorialism.

The reflex user tends to favour a more planned shooting style: the screen encourages picture composition; the increasingly common LED or LCD displays below or alongside the screen turn the finder into what advertising copywriters like to call a command centre.

The rangefinder LEICA on the other hand is less formal — it is after all the spiritual predecessor of today's 35 mm point-and-shoot models. With it you get into closer contact with the subject — in distance as much as in approach. (With pictures of people that has advantages and drawbacks.) The LEICA M models are less intrusive, more compact and above all less noisy than any SLR. We are by now so used to the mirror wallop that we almost miss the soft click of the Leica M shutter. (When I switch to the rangefinder LEICA after using an SLR, I instinctively wait for the missing mirror crash.) The silent shutter action has become legendary: some American judges allow pictures in court only with a LEICA M.

Finally, the Leica M rangefinder is still the most accurate and convenient system of its kind. With most subjects the combined split image and double image is significantly more reliable than the focusing screen, even with its focusing aids. The rangefinder is equally efficient at all lens apertures, quick to use and more visible in poor light than a reflex screen image.

In some respects the SLR has even encouraged a revival of the rangefinder Leica for intimate features. Accustomed to the bulky and noisy SLR, people take less notice when they are being photographed with a Leica M. The photographer quietly shoots frame after frame, not perhaps as rapidly as a motorised SLR, but far less obtrusively.

We are not however concerned with relative efficiency of the SLR and the rangefinder camera — but rather with the special applications of each for specific jobs. In particular, we are concerned with the technical scope of the LEICA M models — right up to the M6.

One point of LEICA engineering is that professionals appreciate the extraordinary mechanical reliability of the LEICA. On the one hand it appears a little old-fashioned among highly automated and motorized cameras with multiple programs, central processing units and other electronic marvels. On the other hand, it is just that electronic wizardry that many professional (especially press) photographers will still view with more than a little suspicion. An electrical fault or a dud battery puts the whole camera out of action. In the LEICA M6 the battery and electronics are relevant only to exposure metering; the rest of the camera goes on operating as before. So of course do the other rangefinder LEICA models.

The current LEICA M system

In view of the applications where the LEICA M is the ideal camera rather than just a usable one — sports and feature photography, candid snapshots etc — the current accessories system of the rangefinder LEICA is more condensed than it used to be. Fifty years ago — before there ever was a 35 mm SLR — Leitz had already produced the first reflex housing. That converted the LEICA into a reflex camera for close-ups, macrophotography, photomicrography and long tele shots. Later the LEICAFLEX and LEICA R4 did a more elegant job of that. In line with Leitz's policy of producing the best possible equipment rather than a compromise even for specialised jobs, the former macro gear and long tele lenses are no longer official components of the LEICA M equipment system.

The current LEICA M lenses cover just those focal lengths where the rangefinder camera is superior or equal to the SLR. These lenses thus range from the ultrawide-angle 21mm to 135 mm tele, and in speed from f/1 to f/2.8.

Lens accessories include bright-line finders for the shortest focal lengths, lens hoods (provided with the lens where not built in initially) and filters.

Further there is a winder for picture sequences, a table-top tripod with ball-and-socket head, a clip-on exposure meter (for the M models without built-in meter) and various camera and holdall cases. We shall come back later to selecting the best outfit.

Dealing with the current LEICA M range in general and with the LEICA M6 in particular, this handbook is a guide to the LEICA style of photography. It is not however a theoretical introduction to photo technique — for basic concepts see appropriate textbooks. As we do need some basic definitions, theoretical points relevant to understanding camera operation are either explained on the spot or summarised in the TECHNICAL GLOSSARY at the end.

The LEICA M6 and M4-P

These two current rangefinder LEICA models differ only in the M6's exposure metering system. In all other respects handling is identical. External differences are the film speed setting dial in the camera back, the flash contacts, the front battery compartment on the M6 and the finder windows.

All Leitz equipment items and accessories, including the camera bodies and lenses, have an order code number. Frequently this is marked on the item itself. Apart from being a catalogue reference, these order codes are often a more reliable designation of the equipment than a description. Where feasible, such order numbers are therefore indicated in square brackets — e.g. [10 404] — whenever this aids identification.

A first impression

Sixty years ago the LEICA was regarded as minute. At roughly 750g (with the standard 50 mm lens) it is today distinctly at the weighty end of current compact 35 mm types. For it still incorporates heavy-duty engineering, not injection-moulded plastic. It is a camera you can get to grips with.

The LEICA M models are rangefinder cameras. That is, they have a precisely aligned viewfinder system built into the top of the camera, marking the field of view taken in by the lens, together with an optical indication that the lens is set to the correct distance for a sharp picture. The round-ended all-metal body further incorporates the shutter, the film track and film transport mechanism.

The LEICA M6 body is available in a black chrome [10 404]or a bright chrome[10414] finish, as is the M4-P [10 415 and 10 416 respectively]. The current preference is for black cameras; earlier LEICA M models were more widely sold in a bright chrome finish. Until about 1970 the black models were black enamelled, not chrome.

The LEICA M models all have a horizontally running focal plane shutter with speeds from 1/1000 sec to 1 sec and a B setting for time exposures.

Special to the M6 is a built-in silicon photodiode which reads the light reflected from a white spot on the first shutter curtain. This is thus selective (large-spot) metering through the lens — a system the LEICA M5 initiated among 35 mm rangefinder cameras. The meter is coupled with

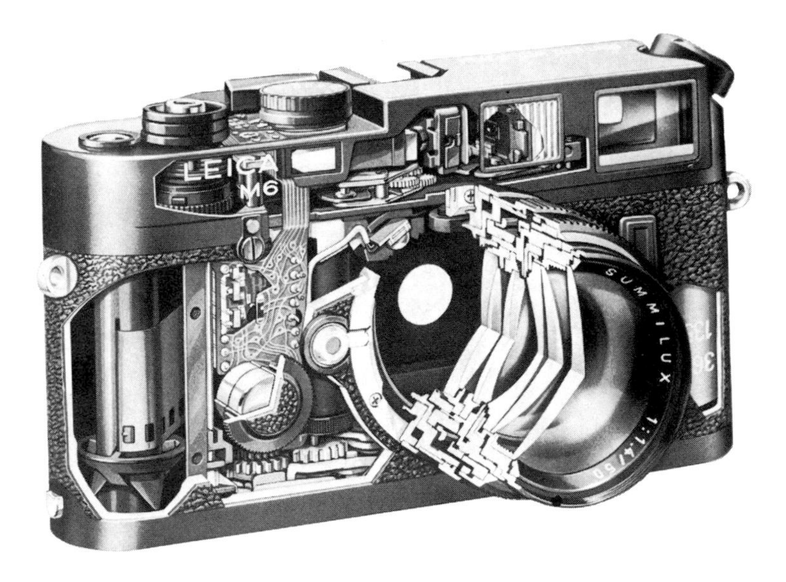

The LEICA M6 (top) incorporates a fair amount of electronics associated with the meter cell (slightly to the left above the white circle on the shutter curtain). The white circle is the metering target for spot readings virtually in the film plane. The electronic system includes the printed circuit just behind the front panel and the cells in the battery compartment.

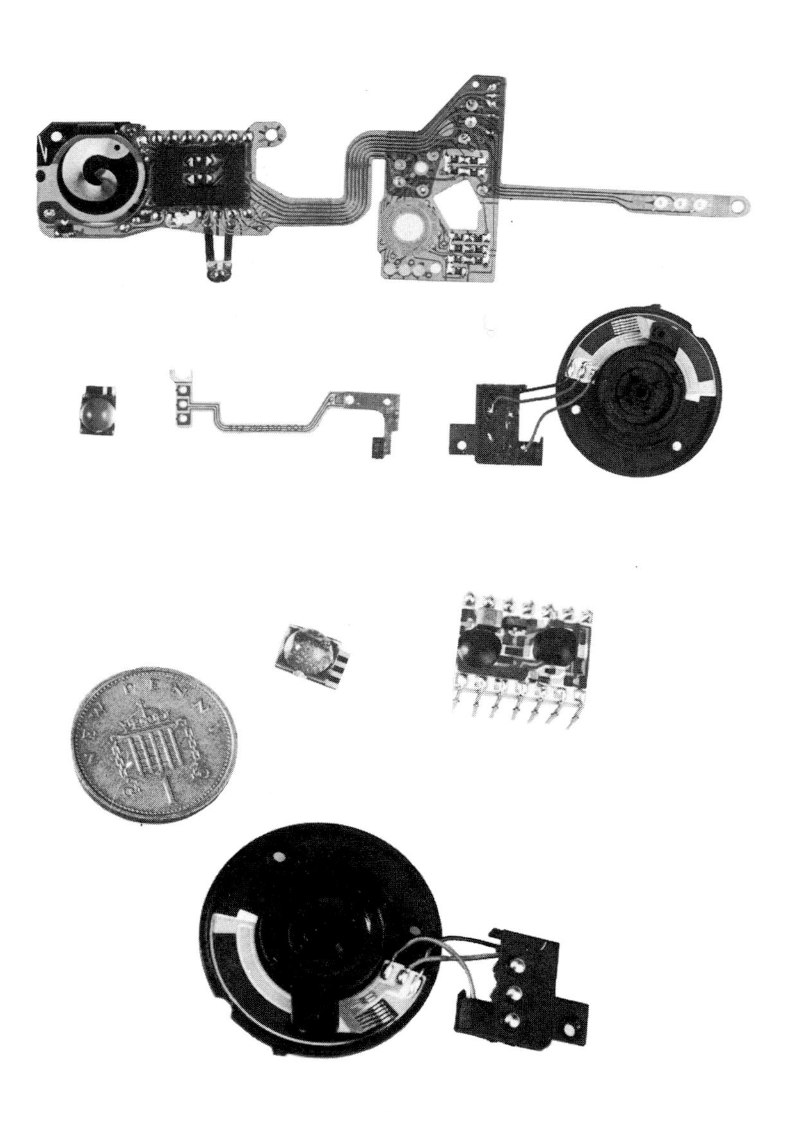

The electronic system (top) consists of a printed circuit with a microprocessor and electric scanning of the shutter speed setting, plus the meter cell, the film setting in the back and contacts between the back and body. The main items (below) are the silicon cell, the microprocessor chip and (once more) the film speed setting contacts. The penny (for scale) is 20 mm in diameter.

Externally the M4-P differs only slightly from the LEICA M6. Apart from the lettering, the only item missing here is the M6's battery compartment on the front.

the shutter speed and film speed settings. When the aperture and shutter speed combination is right for a correct exposure, a pair of LEDs lights up below the finder.

The LEICA LeicaM4-P has no built-in exposure meter, nor do previous M versions other than the M5. However, these models can couple with the accessory Leicameter MR. In all cases the aperture and shutter speed coupling is purely mechanical, independent of any battery. The camera base may be replaced by a winder for exposure sequences. A carrying strap is supplied with the camera.

The controls

In the descriptions of the camera we shall keep talking about 'left' and 'right'; this invariably refers to the camera as held ready to shoot, not to the usual front view. Thus the release button is considered to be at the top right. Seen from the back, the lateral references are correct for the normal view of the camera, from the front for the camera seen upside down.

Let's start at the top, with the inclined re-wind crank — for rewinding the exposed film into its cartridge — at the extreme left. The crank folds out.

Near central on the top is the accessory shoe to take flash units and special viewfinders. Today a standard feature of virtually any 35 mm camera (and many others), this shoe first appeared in Barnack's proto-LEICA. In the M6, M4-P and M4-2 a centre contact in the shoe (hot shoe) is wired directly to the flash synch contact built into the shutter.

To the right of the shoe is the shutter speed dial. It carries engraved reciprocal exposure times in seconds (e.g. 30 = 1/30 sec). The lightning symbol is the shortest time (1/50 sec) for synchronised electronic flash shots.

To the right of the speed dial is the winding lever that advances the film and retensions the shutter after every shot. The lever normally rests against the speed dial, swings out to a start position at about 30° and has a 120° operating throw. You can also operate it in several short swings. In the centre of the lever is the release button; in the M6 slight pressure on this button also switches on the exposure meter circuit. The button carries a standard cable release socket.

Operating controls of the M6 (here with 35 mm lens): the top cover is remarkably uncluttered. At the left is the rewind crank, in the centre the hot shoe and immediately next to it the shutter speed dial. At the far left is the frame counter (here at two divisions before zero) and next to it — in the centre of the winding lever — the release button. The winding lever is shown in its start position. Immediately below it appears the film plane marking.

Between the speed dial and the winding lever (covered by the latter in its rest position) the top carries an engraved circle with a line through it. This is the film plane location — the reference point for the distance scales on the lenses.

The frame counter at the right-hand end of the top, seen through a magnifying lens, counts exposures forward from −2 (2 divisions before 0) to 40.

Looking at the lens (for instance the standard 50mm f/1.4) from the top, as it is mounted on the camera, we have nearest to the camera the fixed depth of field scale spread out to each side of the distance setting index. Further forward is the ribbed focusing ring with distance scales in metres (white) and feet (yellow), then the aperture ring with aperture scale (the ring engages at half stop intervals but can be set to any intermediate value) and finally at the very front a groove to hold the lens hood. The latter is built-in on the longer-focus lenses.
For a front view remove the lens and look at the camera upside down.

In this inverted front view of the camera 'left' and 'right' also refers to the controls to be operated by the left and right hand respectively. Thus in the front the finder frame selector lever appears to the left of the lens, with the chrome bayonet release button for the lens to the right. Above that is the somewhat larger battery compartment cover. The three windows, from left to right, are the viewfinder window, the illuminating window for the finder frames and the rangefinder window. Above the latter is the rewind release clutch.

First of all, there are three windows: the large viewfinder window on the very left, next to it the smaller illuminating window for the finder frames and farther to the right the still smaller rangefinder window. (We shall look at the finder optics in more detail later.)

Next to the rangefinder window is the engraved model designation (M6 — located differently on other models) and below it (still looking at the camera upside down) the rewind clutch lever. This disengages the film transport for rewinding the film.

On the M6 the finder windows are mounted flush with the front of the body and therefore easy to clean. On the M4-P and ealier models the windows are slightly recessed.

Slightly left of centre is the lens opening and flange to take the lens (optical register 27.8 mm). With the lens removed the shutter curtains are visible through the opening; in the M6 also the white spot on the first curtain (provided the camera is tensioned). Just within the flange is the rangefinder coupling lever with a roller that bears on the focusing cam at the rear of the lens. Slightly behind this lever on the M6 the silicon photocell points at the metering spot on the shutter curtain. To the left of the flange (still with the camera seen inverted) is the finder frame selector lever for alternative bright-line finder frames. To the right of the flange a chrome button disengages the bayonet lens lock, further right the M6 has a round battery compartment cover. (The M5, M4 and most earlier models have a selftimer in that position.) The ends of the body carry eyelets for fixing the carrying strap.

Inside the lens flange the roller of the rangefinder coupling lever is visible in the centre and to the left of it the housing of the meter cell, pointing inwards.

The layout of the camera back is supremely simple — with the finder eyepiece at the top left and the coaxial flash socket in the centre, just below the hot shoe. The film speed setting dial is in the centre of the hinged back panel.

The camera base carries only the fold-down opening key at one end and the tripod bush at the other. The base plate is removable for film loading.

Finally, the camera back. With the base plate removed, you can open a hinged flap in the back. The centre of this flap carries the film speed setting dial. In the LEICA M6 the dial is adjustable from ISO 6/9° to 6400/39° and the settings are input electrically into the metering circuit. The M4-P and earlier models have various film speed and type indicators purely as a memory aid.

At the top left is the finder eyepiece, at the top centre a coaxial socket as a second flash synch outlet. Both the synch contacts are so-called X contacts; the M4-P and earlier models have two sockets for electronic flash (X) and flash bulbs (M).

The viewfinder

Finally, before trying out the camera, let's take a brief look through the finder.
It shows the subject at a slightly reduced scale, together with a pair of broken brilliant frames to outline the field of view covered. The frames switch according to the lens on the camera. With for instance the standard 50 mm lens the outer frame is that lens's view, the inner frame the view of the 75 mm lens. This inner frame also appears on the M4-P but not on earlier M models where the 50 mm bright-line frame always stands on its own.

In the very centre of the finder is the range finder area — a small rectangle in which parts of the image at times appear with double outlines.

The LEICA M1 to M5

While the numbering of previous LEICA M models fills the gap up the the M6, it does not run in sequence of appearance — as mentioned before, the M generation started with the LEICA M3 in 1954. Then followed the M2, M1, M4, M5 and some special versions — summarised in the LEICA HISTORY chapter. However, the numerical sequence does reflect a conceptual build-up:

The LEICA M1 was the simplest version, without rangefinder and with bright-line frames for just 35 mm and 50 mm lenses in the viewfinder. It was envisaged less as a cheaper amateur model than as a camera body for scientific and laboratory set-ups (macrophotography, photomicrography, instrument recording etc) where a rangefinder — or any kind of finder — was irrelevant. Eventually Leitz followed this through logically in the finderless MD, MDa and MD-2 models.

The LEICA M2 was meant to be a slightly stripped down and lower-priced alternative to the M3 but the distinction became less significant as originally missing features got added (e.g. the selftimer).

The LEICA M3 — with a larger finder view but fewer finder frames — was the initial flagship of the M range. It also underwent more internal changes than any LEICA M for — inevitably with a new camera design — there were teething troubles, numerous constrution and engineering improvements etc. But the M3 is justifiably the best known M camera, with over 220,000 made.

The LEICA M4 cleaned up some of M3 limitations, adopted the smaller-scale but more versatile M2 finder configuration and replaced the rewind knob by a crank.

The LEICA M4-2 took that further by adding internal coupling elements for a motor winder and a hot shoe but dropping the selftimer (it was in the way for the motor coupling). The M4-P eliminated winder teething troubles and added more finder frames.

The LEICA M5 was Leitz's first attempt to incorporate an internal TTL exposure metering system. However, it made the camera too bulky for many LEICA lovers who indicated that they preferred the smaller M4, even without meter. (In response to that, the M4-2 and M4-P came after the M5.) With the LEICA M6, Leitz solved both the metering and the size problems of the M5.

This logical development improved details but — except for the M5 — changed very little in the camera shape or concept, and even less in handling. Most of this book thus applies equally well to the LEICA M1 to M4. The EARLIER M SYSTEM chapter details main operational differences; minor ones are mentioned in the text as they arise.

Basic Camera Handling

In workmanship and technical features (and also price) the LEICA is very much a professional camera. It is still easy to handle — even for a comparative beginner. However, it is not a point-and-shoot camera. That is also the key to its versatility.

The best way of getting to know the camera is to practise its operation step by step, without a film, to start with.

A few preliminaries: if you acquired the camera new (in a luxurious presentation case), you will want to attach the black woven nylon carrying strap to the eyelets on the body. Adjust the length for convenient carrying over the shoulder or around the neck (see **Using the strap**).

The carrying strap exists in different versions and attachment fittings [current version 14 258]. It is tough and not easy to yank off. There are also straps of other brands in more or less fancy types and designs. If you like carrying the camera underneath a jacket, a strap with a snap hook is useful — you can unclip the camera without taking off the jacket.

Mounting the lens

To mount the lens, remove the latter's rear cap (and the camera's front cap if you haven't just taken another lens off). Place the lens against the camera mount so that the red dot on the lens faces the bayonet release button with its red mark on the camera. Press the lens against the camera and turn clockwise to secure. To remove, press the bayonet release, turn the whole lens anticlockwise to align the red dots again and lift off.

Before changing lenses, fit the front lens cap over the lens; after changing lenses immediately fit the rear cap over the one taken off. The caps protect the glass surfaces against dust and finger prints. It may be a slight bother to fiddle with lens caps every time you change lenses; it is more of a bother having to clean off finger prints all the time. In general, it is better to keep a lens clean than to keep cleaning it. (See also the CAMERA AND LENS CARE chapter.) But remember to remove the cap before shooting!

The standard push-on metal caps offer good protection but do not necessarily stay on securely — for instance when carrying the lens in a pocket. Screw-in caps from various accessories makers are more secure but fiddly. A good compromise is snap-on caps that engage the internal filter thread. (But they are not necessarily available for all filter thread diameters found on LEICA lenses.)

Batteries

For exposure metering the LEICA M6 needs a battery. The battery compartment is behind the round screw cover, next to the lens in the camera front. Use one of the following battery types:

- Two silver oxide cells of 1.5 volts each, international designation SR 07. Specific brand names and types: S76E (Eveready, Ucar); EPX 76 (Ucar); G13 (National and other Japanese brands); V76PX and V76H (Varta); MS76H, 10L14 (Mallory); SR 44F (Maxell); RS76G (Ray-o-Vac). Silver oxide batteries are the most expensive but also the most reliable, especially at low temperatures. The battery voltage remains constant during the whole life of operating the cell — in normal use at least one year per set.
- Alkaline cells of the same size, again of 1.5 volts; usual designation A76 or LR44. Their voltage is not quite as constant and the capacity (and price) is about about half that of a silver oxide battery.
- Lithium cells of 3 volts — type DL 1/3N (Duracell, Mallory) or CR 1/3N (Sanyo, Varta etc). The lithium cell yields twice the voltage of a silver oxide cell and is twice as high; hence one lithium cell replaces two silver oxide one. A lithium cell costs about the same as a pair of silver oxide cells, but has a longer shelf life when not used for extended periods.

Do not use mercury oxide cells. Though of the same size as silver oxide cells (usual designation No. 675 or HC), their 1.35 volts are insufficient for the M6's exposure meter system.

If you are using silver oxide or alkaline batteries insert two cells in the retaining spring of the battery compartment lid — with the flat (+) side up. Alternatively insert a single lithium cell. Then screw the lid with the cells into the compartment at the front.

To ensure good contact remove any traces of grease etc before inserting the cells: wipe them with a clean handkerchief, then avoid touching the front and back with the fingers. If the camera is likely to be out of use for weeks or months, it is preferable to remove the batteries to avoid damage through possible battery leakage. (The risk is greatest with alkaline cells whose leaking chemicals can corrode the contact spring in the battery compartment. Chemicals emerging from silver oxide cells are comparatively harmless and easily wiped off.)

When the batteries are near exhaustion, the exposure metering LEDs become weaker and eventually fail to light. (See EXPOSURE TECHNIQUE chapter.) The meter system does not work either, but without the LEDs it would be useless anyway.

Always change batteries in complete sets. Combining a fresh with a nearly spent cell increases the leakage risk. Also don't combine alkaline and silver oxide cells.

As batteries are liable to fail quite abruptly, it is a good idea to carry a set of spare cells, for instance in the small leather container that buttons onto the carrying strap [14 258]. (This takes silver oxide or alkaline cells but not lithium ones.)

Apart from the M5, no other LEICA M model needs batteries.

Finally, for a trial run with the M6 set a film speed. For the moment turn the centre portion of the film speed setting dial (in the camera back) so that the arrow heads are vertical — i.e. point to 24° and 200.

The trial run

These are the operating steps for taking a picture:

(1) Preparation: Swing out the transport lever to its start position (and operate it if the shutter is not tensioned). Remember to remove the lens cap!! (I usually put it in my pocket at the start of a shooting session.)

(2) Set the aperture and shutter speed (more about that in the EXPOSURE TECHNIQUE chapter). Turn the shutter speed dial to 125 and very slightly depress the release button: A red arrowhead LED (or pair of LEDs) should appear in the finder. (If they don't, either the shutter is not tensioned or the lens cap is still on the lens.) Aim the camera to centre the rangefinder window on a representative subject area. Turn the lens aperture ring in the direction of the arrowhead LED in the finder until the second LED lights up opposite the first one, with equal brightness. (The first LED must not go out.) This sets the correct exposure with normal daylight subjects (or indoors with the LEICA pointing at a window). If the LED goes out during all this, briefly touch the release button again.

(3) Focus: Turn the ribbed focusing ring on the lens (the ring with the distance scale) until the double subject outlines visible in the central rangefinder field of the finder fuse into one.

(4) Release: Once you have the subject framed the way you want it (within the right bright-line frame for the lens used), smoothly press the release button. Keep the camera steady. Look for additional support where possible.

(5) Advance the film: Pull out the winding lever as far as it will go. This advances the film by one frame and also retensions the shutter.

Some photographers wait with winding until just before the next shot — that avoids the risk of accidental releasing. But if you wind after every shot, you are always ready for the next one and handling is more consistent. If you sometimes have the camera tensioned and decide not to expose after all, you never know whether the camera is ready to shoot or not. So it's better to wind immediately after every exposure.

You can work the winding lever either in one full 120° swing or in several short ones. A full pull is quicker — but with some camera holds the short pulls are convenient as you don't have to change the hold of the right hand.

The steps themselves are simple enough. But certain practical and technical points are involved, too. The practical aspects are a correct camera hold (and releasing), the technical ones cover the how and why of focusing (step 3) and exposure (step 2).

Avoiding camera shake

LEICA lenses yield outstanding definition. Yet not every picture is as sharp as it ought to be. One cause may be camera shake. The camera moved slightly during the exposure. The longer the exposure time, the greater risk of camera shake — for while the shutter runs down and uncovers the film, any movement of the image projected on the film blurs the picture.

The primary remedy against camera shake is to use a short enough exposure time (fast shutter speed). That's why we set $^1/_{125}$ sec for the trial run. With a moderately steady camera hold that ensures shake-free shots. Where poor light or other conditions call for slower shutter speeds, use special release techniques to minimise shake.

Holding the camera steady

In the first place that means a steady camera hold. For horizontal shots — the most obvious way with that camera shape — grip the right end of the camera with the right hand so that the body rests against the centre of the palm and is also supported by the little finger. Press the middle and ring fingers against the camera front, place the thumb behind the winding lever (swung out to its start position) and rest the right index finger on the release button. The right hand end of the carrying strap can run either between the middle and index fingers or in front of the index finger. (But running it downwards in the palm is uncomfortable.) This hold also locates the operating functions of the right hand: the index finger does the releasing and the thumb advances the film. If necessary, extend the index finger further to adjust shutter speeds on the speed dial.

The left index finger and thumb grip the focusing ring of the lens from underneath. If needed they can also switch to the aperture ring to select alternative apertures. The left ring and little fingers again support the camera from underneath.

The normal camera hold for horizontal shots, here with right-eye viewing. The strap, wound round the right wrist and running round the back of the neck, provides additional support.

Which eye for viewing? As the eyepiece is at the left, you can easily view with the left eye. The forehead then supports the top rear camera edge and — if you don't have too big a head — still allows convenient operation of the winding lever. If you see better with the right eye, support the left-hand camera end against the right-hand side of the nose.

Upright hold, again for right-eye viewing. Preferably have the right hand on top.

For upright shots swing the right hand up (without changing its grip on the camera) and support the left-hand camera end in the left hand, This — as for horizontal shots — again operates the aperture and focusing rings on the lens. This is easiest when viewing with the left eye as you can then press the camera back against the forehead. Right-eye viewing is less comfortable in this case as the rear edge of the top cover presses against your right eyebrow. Unless you are using the winder, an upright hold with the right hand below is still less convenient as you would in that case have to operate the release with the right thumb and change you grip to advance the film.

These camera holds need some modification with wide-angle lenses on the one hand and long-focus ones on the other. The wide-angle lenses have a focusing lever attached to the distance ring, within easy reach of the left index or middle finger. (The current verson of the 50 mm SUMMICRON f/2 has such a lever, too.) So push or pull this lever for focusing — and use the left index finger also to push the aperture ring as required. The support for the camera is a trifle less steady with these lenses; preferably push the left thumb and middle finger against the side and bottom of the camera. (That also applies to upright shots.)

With the longer focal lengths the focusing ring is located further forward; use the thumb and the index or middle fingers of the left hand to operate it. The other fingers also move forward and partly support the camera directly below the lens. Keep the fingers of the left hand clear of the finder window. (The middle finger of the right hand may also stray in front of the rangefinger — but you immediately notice that by the loss of the rangefinder image.)

The correct stance also counts. Try to lean against something solid — a wall, tree etc. If no such support is available, stand with the feet slightly apart and tuck the elbows into your sides for better support.

Other ways of steadying the camera include supporting the elbows on railings, a low wall, a table top, the arms of a chair (when seated). Or, when sitting on the floor, support the elbows on your knees. In every case, the steadier the support, the less the risk of camera shake. The table stand (see **Tripod support**) provides further ways of steadying the camera.

On the other hand, avoid leaning against, or supporting the camera on, any part of a moving vehicle from which you are shooting. Such movement is invariably linked with vibration — and that should not be transferred to the camera. Preferably stand free, possibly with slightly bent knees so that the body becomes its own vibration damper. This applies equally when shooting on board ship (the engine vibration is insiduous but nonetheless camera shaking), from aircraft or — especially — from helicopters. If you have to shoot in such circumstances, use the fastest possible shutter speed. (Professionals photographing from helicopters sometimes use special vibration dampening camera mountings.)

Using the strap

The camera strap is of course for carring the camera. But it also provides additional steadying support. For shooting readiness you must be able to get the camera quickly up to eye level. There are three ways of using the strap:

(a) Run it round the neck, with the camera on the chest. You are instantly ready to shoot — and instantly recognisable from a mile off as a typical photographer/tourist.
(b) Hang the strap and camera over one shoulder (usually the right). The anti-slip pad inhibits it from riding down. In this position the camera is less conspicuous — yet you can still raise it quickly to shoot. However it is also easier to lose — or to be torn off by passing motorcycle bandits. The camera is better protected and still less conspicuous if you carry it underneath a jacket which hides it until you are ready to shoot.
(c) With the strap running round the neck and diagonally across the chest, the LEICA is still more secure and — if the strap is long enough — still easy to raise to the eye. Here, too, you can hide the camera under a jacket.

Carried over the right shoulder, the camera is always ready to shoot. You can carry it like this under a jacket, too.

Getting the strap length right for the camera over the shoulder: suspended from the hand it should dangle just below the elbow.

The optimum strap length depends of course on your own size. Adjust the strap until it gives the best support with your selected camera hold but is still easy to carry comfortably. Removing the camera is easier with a divided strap and a snap hook: unhook it and pull out the free strap end — even from underneath your jacket.

A rule of thumb — or perhaps of elbow — for strap length for the first two holds. Let the camera dangle on the strap from the base of your thumb while you hold your arm out straight. Bend the lower arm up at the elbow: the camera should now hang just below the elbow.

For the third way of carrying the camera — (c) above — the strap must of course be longer. In this case raise the camera to your eye so that the strap runs from the left eyelet over the left shoulder, round your back and below the right arm, ending between the right thumb and index finger. If you use your left eye for viewing and the strap is of the right length, you can support the camera against your forehad as described before. Pushing down the right arm and pressing your head forward against the camera tensions the strap so that the camera, your right hand and head form an almost rigid unit. You get a similarly rigid unit with an upright hold. (This way of supporting the camera is not quite so convenient for right-eyed viewing.)

Pictorial colour contrast. Complementary colours enhance each other's luminosity. The dark background in this shot also helped. *Photo: Dr M. Beisert.*

If the camera is hanging just round your neck, push up your right hand underneath the strap — before raising the camera to your eye — and wind the strap once round the right wrist. That shortens the strap to bring the camera close to the face. Bring the left hand over the strap to grip the camera; this tensions the strap further. Once more, get the camera, your head and two hands to form a rigid block. This is easier, too, for right-eyed viewing (but still better with the left eye).

With the camera hanging over the right shoulder (over or under a jacket) raising it to the eye is easier still. In this case the strap should run from the right-hand camera end under the right arm, forward over the shoulder and up underneath the camera to the left strap eyelet. If the length is right, the strap braces the right arm and the camera for a steady hold. The left strap end must run underneath the camera as it would otherwise be in the way of the nose.

This support is suitable for left-eyed or right-eyed viewing, but again is more convenient with the left. The strap under the camera slightly interferes with the hold of the left hand. On the other hand the tensioning frame formed by the strap and the right hand does not really need additional left hand support — you can use that hand to operate directly the aperture and focusing rings on the lens.

Shooting readiness is vital for pictures of children. With a right camera hold you should be able to manage hand-held snapshots even with longer lenses. The most impressive child shots capture passing expressions — but the camera must be ready, too.

Photo: Dr M. Beisert.

Smooth releasing

The purpose of all these elaborate ways of supporting the camera is to keep it as steady as possible during that fraction of a second while the shutter is open for the exposure. That whole effort is in vain if you jog the LEICA while you press the release.

The best way of avoiding that is to provide counter pressure. If the right end of the camera is lodged firmly against your palm, the index finger only has to depress the button. Press down from above — avoid tilting the camera either forward or back. The release travel of about 1.5 mm or 1/16 in. is very short — yet when you press slowly it seems incredibly long. The release of the M6 has a first pressure point at about 0.5 mm (the exposure meter is switched on here), then moves a further 0.8 mm before triggering the shutter. (There may be minute variations between cameras.) The first pressure point is less distinct on the M4-P and earlier models.

When you raise the camera to shoot, the strap tensioned around the shoulder provides extra support.

Carrying the camera with the strap around the neck and shoulder is more secure, though a little less comfortable.

Two ways of releasing: with the tip of the index finger (top) and with the first finger joint (bottom). In both cases the cup surrounding the release button supports the index finger.

The correct way of releasing is to depress the button to the point immediately before it trips the shutter, so that for the exposure itself you only have to depress the last fraction of a mm. Preferably practise this — depressing the button just to this holding point soon becomes instinctive. The very last pressure should then be totally smooth, never jerky.

There are two ways of depressing: with the tip of the finger and with the first finger joint. In the latter case the fingertip rests on the shutter, speed dial (and can turn this to change the speed setting). Then depress the release button by straightening the first finger joint to push down. This way is particularly shakeproof but only comfortable with a horizontal camera hold.

You cannot release smoothly after heavy exertion, for instance if you have arrived out of breath at the intended viewpoint. Better wait half a minute before shooting. By all means hold your breath while releasing — but only at the last instant, not for half a minute beforehand.

Oddly enough, steady releaing is even easier with the thumb — useful when 'stealing' unobtrusive shots from waistlevel (with a wide-angle lens).

Tripod support

With practice (and additional support where feasible) shake-free exposures are possible down to about 1/30 sec. Some people even manage to hold the camera steady for up to 1/8 sec. But a solid support is better still.

A firm base is a good start, for instance placing the camera on a table top, a wall etc. More versatile is a table tripod with a ball-and-socket head (ball head for short), for you can set it up almost anywhere and level (or incline) the camera at will.

One of the most stable types for this purpose is the Leitz table stand [10 100] with the large ball head [14 110 or — in an earlier version — 14 121]. For horizontal shots this combination supports the LEICA about 9½ in. above whatever it stands on. When folded up and with the ball head unscrewed, the table tripod fits in an odd pocket of the camera bag. (The smaller head [14 119] takes even less space but is not so rigid.)

When setting up, align the longest of the tripod legs underneath the camera to keep the setup from toppling over. Screw the head firmly to the tripod and the camera firmly to the ball head, then line up the camera precisely while looking through the finder and tighten the clamping lever. If the camera was correctly balanced it will then also stand firmly. Preferably release with a cable release screwed into the release button; that should permit shake-free time exposures of many seconds (at the B setting).

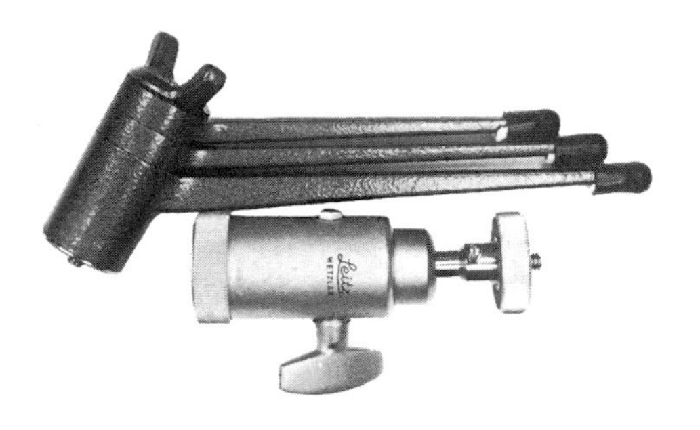

The Leitz table tripod with large ball head can go in a pocket. (I have been using this older version of the ball head for over twenty years.

Table tripod, here with 90 mm lens, set up for horizontal and for upright shots. Note the tripod leg running below the lens to stop the assembly from tipping over.

To stop losing the rubber feet of the tripod legs either jam them on with additional paper wedges or do without the rubbers. But in that case don't place the tripod on easily scratched polished furniture.

Interiors in churches and other poorly lit locations call for a solid large tripod — a nuisance to carry, especially with a 35 mm camera outfit. (In museums tripods — and flash for that matter — are usually banned.) Here I often use the camera mounted on the table tripod and press the latter against a wall, a column or the like. That way I often manage shake-free exposures of several seconds.

The same combination can become a chestpod. Support the three tripod legs against the chest, adjust the camera (with the ball head slack) for convenient location against your viewing eye and clamp tight. The right hand now presses the whole assembly against your body (and presses the release) while the left focuses. Such a hold is particularly useful in the circus or theatre where you are bound to a seat but want to shoot with longer lenses.

With the camera supported against the chest in this way, you can easily manage shots at 1/30 sec, even with a 135 mm lens.

For a steadier hold the table tripod can also become a chestpod.

By supporting the LEICA against a wall the table tripod permits even time exposures up to several seconds. (Useful for interiors, for instance in churches.)

A recent Leitz item is a universal hand grip with shoulder support [14 239] which can serve as a camera support and even as a table tripod. It is however primarily intended for the extreme tele lenses of the SLR LEICA models; with the M6 (and other M models) the table tripod and ball head described above are more convenient and more flexible.

Film Handling

From Oskar Barnack photographers inherited not only the thrill of 35 mm photography but also the fiddly 35 mm film cartridge. At the time perforated motion picture film had the finest emulsion grain on the market. To load it as compactly as possible in his prototype camera, Barnack chose a light-tight cartridge from which the film was fed out and into which it would be spooled back. Film makers soon provided the cartridge packs — but the elaborate loading and unloading procedure remained standard for these last sixty years.

Even the familiar trimmed film leader was Barnack's doing. In the original LEICA the film was loaded edgeways from the camera base; trimming the beginning of the film to a half-width tongue made that part easier to handle.

LEICA M models are still loaded from the camera bottom. But part of the back is now hinged to facilitate film insertion and checking the correct film location. It was the modern LEICA. too, which greatly simplified film threading — not just simpler than with the first LEICA models but easier than with most other 35 mm cameras. The film still needs the usual trimmed leader; nowadays this is about 4 cm or 1½ in. long (rather than the 10 cm it used to be).

Film loading

Loading the film is simple, but you must know how. Preferably practise with a dummy film — or buy the cheapest 24-exposure film to sacrifice on a few trial runs. Film loading is one of those operations you should be able to do instinctively and without looking — you may have to change films in a dark theatre auditorium. Incidentally, never load a film in bright sunlight — at least do it in the shade of your own body.

Here are the steps:

(1) Open the camera base and swing open the back panel.
(2) Start pushing the film cartridge into the cartridge chamber and the film leader into the film channel.
(3) Check correct engagement of the film leader in the takeup spool core.*
(4) Push the back panel against the body, refit the base plate and secure.
(5) Advance the film to the first frame.
(6) Set the film speed.

* M1,2,3 loading differs, see page 23

To load the film, push the cartridge with its protruding film leader into the cartridge chamber and the film channel respectively so that the film end extends into one of the take-up spool slots (below). The diagram in the camera base shows the recommended film path.

Applies to M4, M4-2, M4-P and M6.

The baseplate lock is at the left-hand camera end. Raise the key and turn by half a turn to the left. (Earlier LEICA M cameras had 'open — auf' and 'close — zu' markings around the key to show which way to turn it.) Then pull off the baseplate at the key end and disengage from the retaining stud at the other end.

Obviously you want to load a film into an empty camera. Opening the baseplate of a loaded camera will fog the film. So check first (if you haven't just unloaded the LEICA): by unfolding the rewind crank and turning in the direction of the arrow. If it turns completely freely, the camera is empty.

A convenient way of loading is to place the camera on a table in front of you, upside down and with the open back facing you. But you can do it in your lap, too. Keep the separate baseplate handy — but don't put it on the floor where it could pick up dust.

With the right hand hold the cartridge above the film compartment at the right of the camera and pull out the film leader far enough to reach across to the takeup spool core with its three spikes. Push the cartridge into the compartment so that the film slides into the film channel and the beginning of the leader runs into one of the spool slots. The diagram inside the open camera base shows how the film should run.

At this point you can really close the back and replace the base plate. Push the back firmly against the body, engage the tongue of the base with its hole in the stud on the camera bottom at the left, pull it fully over the body at the other end and lock with the folding key. Fully pull out the winding lever (press the release if necessary). Then tension the film slightly with the rewind crank (till you feel a resistance), press the release again and advance once more. During this second operation of the winding lever the rewind crank should turn against the direction of its arrow — to show that the film is advancing correctly. If the crank does not turn, wind the film again, release and wind once more. If the crank still fails to turn, the film was not properly attached to the take-up core; so open the camera and reload the film.

The fastidious way is to check correct film location between the outer film track rails before closing the back. If necessary adjust the film position. During the first transport cycle check also whether the spool core is pulling the film along. Normally the wheel flange in the base plate pushes the film into its correct position in the film track. What counts is that the film advances — otherwise you are liable to make all 36 shots on the film leader. (It happened to me once — since then I pay special attention to correct film transport at the beginning.)

This is how the film then winds up on the take-up spool — inside the closed camera of course (here open to show the film run).

Applies to M4, M4-2, M4-P and M6.

Occasionally the film may slip out of the take-up spool core, so that the rewind crack rotates only during the first transport cycle. Check the crank movement till at least the second frame. If the film fails to advance, open the camera and insert the film afresh. If during this stage you pulled out more film from the cartridge, advance on loading to at least frame No.2 (or even 3) before you start shooting.

If you hear a scraping sound inside the camera, that may be the film perforations riding over the transport sprocket — a sure sign that the film has left the take-up core, for the sprocket is not carrying the film with it.

The ideal film path for reliable engagement is that shown in the diagram in the base. Threading the film through two slots of the spool core does not really help — if anything the film may slip off the spool even more easily. In cold weather especially avoid pushing in the film too far — as it is then more brittle it may break more easily when strongly bent. And bits of film debris stuck in the film gate could be disastrous.

If the base plate proves difficult to close you either failed to push the film cartridge fully home into its chamber (slightly turn the rewind crank to make it engage in the cartridge spool core) or you accidentally turned the base plate key to its closed position before fitting it on the camera. (In the open position the key cannot fold down.)

The alternate advancing and releasing sequence not only advances the frame counter to No.1 but also brings a fresh unexposed section of the film from the cartridge into the film gate.

The back open for checking the film location; in the M6 it carries contacts to input the film speed setting into the camera.

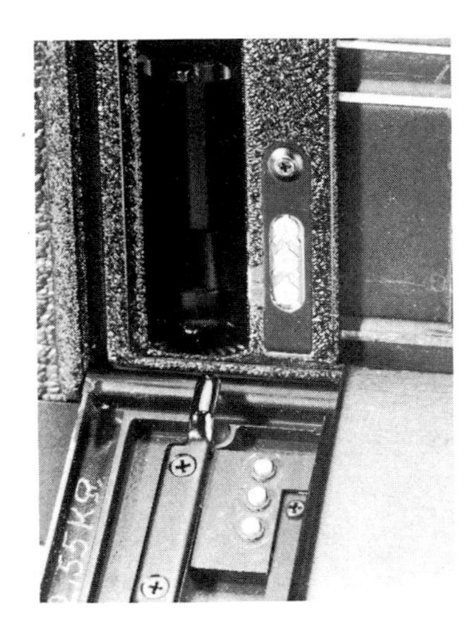

Finally set the film speed in the camera back. Turn the film speed dial with a finger so that the arrow heads point to the required speed in arithmetic (lower scale) or logarithmic (upper scale) ISO values. The film packing and, nearly always, the film cartridge indicate the speed. The speed dial setting inputs this value into the M6's exposure metering system.

On the M4-P write the film data on the white film memo panel in the centre of the indicator in the camera back. The scale surrounding this shows comparative ASA and DIN values (forerunners of the current ISO scale and numerically the same as the latter). Earlier LEICA M models have a settable scale but — as on the M4-P — this is a pure memory aid.

Reloadable cartridges

Current 35 mm film is sold almost exclusively in prefilled cartridges of 24 or 36 exposures, ready for loading into the camera. Some special films are also available in bulk lengths of 10 or 30 m (33 or 100 feet). These you cut into lengths (1.65 m for 36 exposures) to load into a film cartridge in total darkness. Two types of cartridge may be involved: rechargeable standard cartridges and the Leitz N cassette.

Rechargeable cartridges available commercially are similar to the normal cartridges in which films are sold, but are easier to open and to close without damage. (Some cartridge makes — such as Kodak — are intended to be used once only and are ruined on opening.) There are also film loaders that take up to 30 m of bulk film; apart from the initial charging with film all further loading operations can run in daylight.

The type N Leitz cassette |14 006| — no longer made but possibly still found among older stock of some photo shops — consists of a spool like that of a regular cartridge plus an outer and an inner shell between which the film runs in a light-tight channel. The cassette fits all LEICA M models (other than M5). The cassette opens inside the camera as you close the baseplate lock. This rotates the shells against each other to open a wide slot so that the film runs freely without risk of scratching.

If you plan to reload your own cartridges, then preferably sacrifice a film (for example the one used for loading practice) to dismantle the cartridge. Observe the exact film orientation and layout. Note that the film is wound emulsion in, that it unwinds clockwise as seen from the spool knob end and that the longer edge of the trimmed film leader is alongside the spool knob when the film is wound up.

To recharge a cartridge from a loader, attach the film end protruding from the loader to the cartridge spool with adhesive tape. Run the latter from the rear of the film round the spool core and to the front so that the tape adheres to both sides of the film. Assemble the cartridge, place it in the light-tight spooling chamber of the loader, close the chamber and wind the film (through the cartridge slit) onto the spool.

After loading, trim the film leader, using the spoilt practice film as a guide. The leader should be about 2 in. long and at the most 1 in. wide. Take care not to cut through perforation holes.

You can even reload some commercial cartridges if you first remove all traces of the previous film (and its securing tape) from the cartridge spool. But in practice the flimsier cartridges tend to warp on opening and are then no longer light-tight. Repeated reloading also accumulates dust and grit in the velvet light trapping of the cartridge slot and can scratch the film. That risk is present with all reloadable cartridges other than the type N Leitz cassette.

Unloading

Once the film is fully exposed it must be rewound into its cartridge. A sure sign that the film is finished is that the winding lever blocks. At this point never use force — that could tear the perforation or even the whole film and ruin it. If you have films processed by a photofinisher (especially colour slide film) preferably write off the last exposure (just before the transport lever blocked), and repeat it on the next film. Photofinishing labs usually splice films together in to endless lengths for running them through automatic processing machines. The very last frame on a film is liable to be the splicing area.

The frame counter can in fact count on to No. 40. However, with a standard 36-exposure film it rarely gets beyond No. 37 — and that is usually that last frame, the one you cannot rely on.

Rewinding is straightforward and a bore. Swing down the rewind clutch lever on the camera front (below and to one side of the rangefinder window) to 'R', unfold the rewind crank and turn clockwise (in the direction of its arrow) until you suddenly feel a reduced winding resistance. An audible scraping noise signals that the film leader has left the take-up spool. Now turn the crank by one further turn (no more), remove the base plate and open the back. The film leader should now be in the film gate. Ease it out downwards, bringing the cartridge with it.

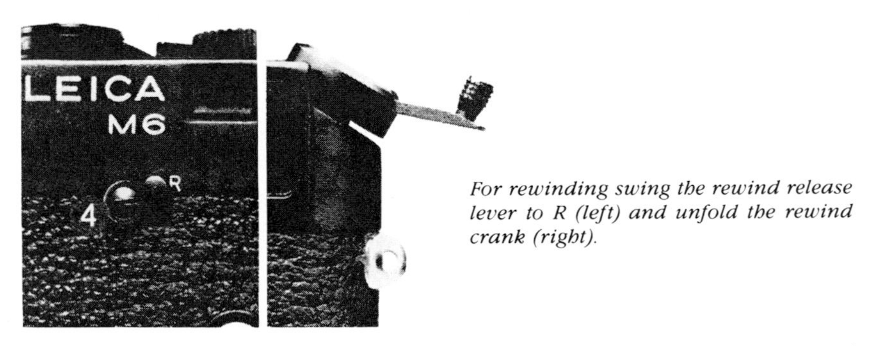

For rewinding swing the rewind release lever to R (left) and unfold the rewind crank (right).

Rewinding a 36-exposure film needs about 30 turns of the rewind crank, 24 exposures need 20-21 turns.

There are arguments for and against winding the film fully back into its cartridge. If the film end still protrudes from the cartridge slot, removal is easier in the way just described. Without this bit of film leader to get hold of, you have to try pulling the cartridge out of its compartment by the spool knob — tricky for those with big fingers. Tapping the camera down on your palm to make the cartridge drop out is not good if the cartridge lands on the floor. With a waterproof felt pen you can also write exposure information on this leader. If you don't write anything on it you may later wonder whether the film was exposed or not — if the leader is wound fully back, there is no doubt.

Is the cartridge more light-tight with or without a protruding film leader? That's open to argument — but should be relevant only if you leave the cartridge lying in the sun — definitely not recommended practice. In fact, unload the film in the shade if at all possible and immediately wrap it up light-tight. The original (nowadays plastic) film can is fine for that; I prefer using plastic slide boxes in which Kodak (and some other film makers) send back processed slides. When covered with black adhesive film, these boxes are reasonably light-tight and hold four cartridges in less space than four separate film cans. When going through airport security checks I pocket these boxes with my films to avoid X-raying (which affects all films). Posso now has similar boxes for three cartridges in a radiation-protective plastic. (But I still prefer to avoid X-raying altogether.)

Partly exposed films

Don't wind the film back fully if you unload a partly exposed film and intend to reload it later — for instance to switch in mid-film from prints to slides or from an ISO 64 material to ISO 400. Professionals rarely do that — they either carry two camera bodies for the two film types or they unload the partly exposed film and waste the unused frames. (On an assignment there is rarely time to fiddle with reloading partly exposed films.)

Here is how to do it if film economy is important: After the last exposure (and after advancing the film) note the number on the frame counter. Rewind the film, keeping the leader outside the cartridge, and write this number on the film leader. For reloading proceed in the usual way but cover the lens with the lens cap while advancing the film to the first frame. Still with the lens cap in place, keep releasing the shutter and advancing the film until the frame counter shows one number higher than the number you noted — then carry on taking pictures. If for instance the frame counter shows No. 18 when you unloaded the film, advance it after reloading to No. 19 before you start taking further pictures. That keeps last exposure of the first run clear of the first shot of the second.

Which film?

Photo industry statistics suggest that around three-quarters of 35 mm film users load their camera with colour print (negative) film, one-fifth with colour slide film and the rest with black-and-white. (Proportions vary a little around the world.)

Negative film yields colour prints to carry in your wallet and show around — and also big enlargements. It is most popular among snapshooters but professionals like it, too. Colour slide film yields colour transparencies for projection; on the screen these appear exceptionally brilliant and sharp (if properly focused and exposed) and come closest to conveying the effect of the original subject or scene. On the other hand they need more elaborate viewing preparations — setting up a projector, blacking out the room etc. The pursuit of that top quality thus calls for some dedication; so slide users tend to be more advanced amateurs.

The choice of the film type — print or slide — thus depends primarily on the intended use of the image. While you can have prints made from slides, you get better quality in prints from negatives. You can even have slides made from negatives, though there is less demand for that facility and fewer photofinishers offer it. Generally slide film is the material for top image quality (that's when professionals use it, too), and print film for snapshots on the one hand and big enlargements on the other.

Black-and-white has long ceased to be the low-cost alternative to colour. Photo dealers and finishers often charge more rather than less for black-and-white prints. Black-and-white is nowadays more a medium for special effects that depend on monochrome reproduction, or for applications (e.g newspaper reproduction) limited to black-and-white images. Nearly all current black-and-white films yield negatives for enlargements.

All three groups include films of various speeds but also of other differences in characterists.

Extreme-speed films, usually of ISO 800/30° to 1600/33°, are almost exclusively intended for poor-light shooting — night, bad weather — or for sports photography where fastest shutter speeds are vital. Usually these are colour films whose effective speed may be boosted further by push-processing — sometimes up to ISO 3200. That may sacrifice colour saturation and fineness of grain. Grain is sometimes utilised pictorially for special effects.

In daylight, extreme-speed films can raise over-exposure problems by being too fast. In bright sunlight an ISO 1600 film would need a shutter speed of $^1/_{4000}$ sec — a quarter of the shortest exposure possible with the LEICA — even at the smallest f/16 aperture of the standard lens.

High-speed films of ISO 200 to 400 are to all intents and purposes universal materials, especially ISO 200. They exist both as print and as slide film. They are on the one hand fast enough for many poor light subjects and on the other can still cope with brightest light conditions. In recent years makers have immensely improved the performance of both slide and print films in this group. Black-and-white emulsions of this speed range are usually ISO 400. A limitation with outdoor shots is that you can rarely use large apertures for deliberately restricted depth of field.

Medium-speed films of ISO 64 to 125 are fine-grain emulsions of high acutance and thus specially suitable for slide projection at high magnification and for giant enlargements from negatives. Most films in this group are around ISO 100; best-known exceptions include Kodachrome 64 (ISO 64 slide film) and Ilford FP4 (black-and-white, ISO 125). These films are less suitable for interiors and low light, but are fine for all subjects not requiring high speed.

Ultrafine-grain films are again a special group (ISO 25 to 50) which today includes a few colour slide films (e.g. Kodachrome 25, Agfachrome 50, Fuji 50) and certain black-and-white materials. They are high-resolving emulsions of specially fine grain whose advantages are however noticeable only in greatly enlarged prints or slides. Their low speed limits general use to subjects in good light.

Rangefinder Technique

The current LEICA is the top rangefinder camera. It has one of the brightest, most accurate and most convenient finders of this kind — for viewing as well as for focusing.

The finder itself is a bright-line or brilliant-frame viewfinder. On looking through it you see a slightly reduced (0.72×) view of the subject. Apparently projected into the scene are frame marks that outline the actual view covered by different interchangeable lenses. A mask plate installed inside the finder selectively uncovers the frame marks. Inserting a lens (between 28 and 135 mm) automatically selects an appropriate viewfinder frame. You can also select frames manually by the frame selector lever on the camera front, within easy reach of the left hand.

The frames appear in pairs:

(a) With 28 mm and 90 mm lenses the bright lines outline a large frame (view of the 28 mm lens) and markings covering a much smaller frame (90 mm).

(b) With 35 mm and 135 mm lenses you see parts of a slightly smaller outer frame (35 mm lens view) and corner marks of a very small inner frame (135 mm) surrounding the rangefinder field.

(c) With the standard and the 75 mm lenses the finder shows markers of a medium large frame (view covered by the 50 mm lens) and a little inside that, corner and edge markings outlining the coverage of the 75 mm lens.

You see the 28 mm and 90 mm frames also with the 21 mm lens. The camera finder cannot however cover the view taken in by this extreme wide-angle lens and you need a supplementary finder (see THE LENS RANGE.)

Irrespectively of the lens fitted, the frame selector lever can also make any pair of frames appear:

- Lever pushed outwards: 35 mm and 135 mm frames
- Lever centred (normal position): 50 mm and 75 mm frames
- Lever pushed inwards: 28 mm and 90 mm frames.

Today's extreme-speed colour films permit hand-held shots in poor light and with fast enough shutter speeds to avoid camera shake even with long-focus lenses. Photo: Dr M. Breisert.

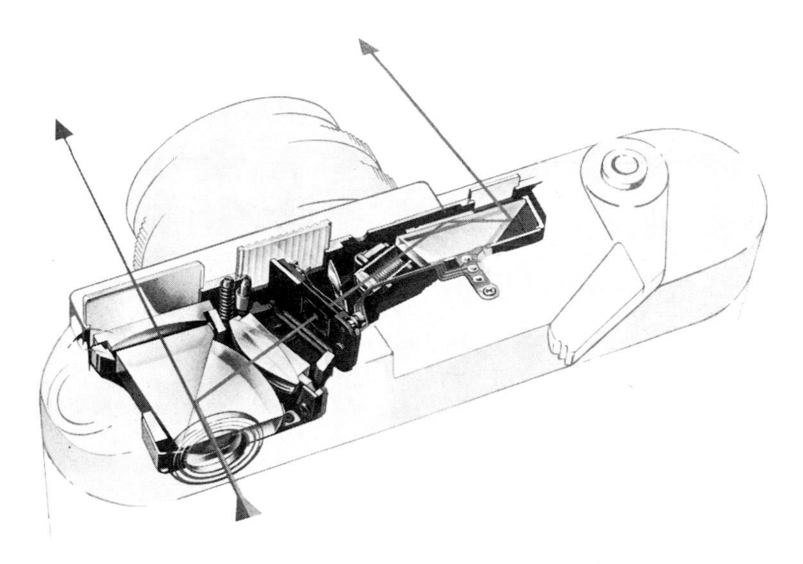

Rangefinder assembly of the LEICA M6 (top) and its optical path (bottom). Clearly visible at the top is the roller that bears on the lens's focusing cam and in the centre the mask plate with its multiple masks and the LED circuit.

For details of the viewfinder frames provided on earlier M camera see the chapter THE EARLIER M SYSTEMS.
With the 50 mm lens the frame selector lever is normally upright. Pull it outwards or push it in as required. With a 28 mm (or a 90mm) lens on the camera, the lever points inwards and you pull it outwards in two stages for the other frame pairs. The reverse applies with 35 and 135 mm — that is also the lever position without a lens on the camera. When

Available-light photography covers exposures by very weak daylight or prevailing artificial light (other than flash). That calls for high-speed lenses and films.

Configuration differences of the inner frame of each pair aid identification. A small frame with only corner marks is the 135 mm frame (and goes with the 35 mm one); a small frame of thin edge marks indictates 90 mm (associated with 28 mm), while the 50/75 mm combination is unmistakable, anyway. With a little practice you note these differences subconsciously.

The finder frame selector helps to preselect the best lens — you can quickly try different fields of view before actually changing lenses.

Finder accuracy and parallax

The optical finder is far more compact than an SLR finder screen — but has two drawbacks: finder parallax and loss of image field. Both affect finder accuracy. The LEICA largely compensates but cannot completely eliminate them.

Seen from behind, the finder is somewhat above and to the left of the lens. Its viewpoint is displaced upwards and sideways by some 35 mm. That is viewfinder parallax. The film always takes in 35 mm less at the side and at the top of the subject than is visible in the finder. As with medium to distance scenes the field is already many yards high and wide, such a shift in coverage is negligible there. But in close-ups — for instance with the 280 × 420 mm field of the standard lens at its nearest focusing distance — the parallax error becomes noticeable. The bright-line frame marks in the LEICA M viewfinder are coupled with the focusing movement: at near distances the frame marks shift diagonally down to the right to compensate for parallax. The residual perspective difference between the finder and the lens's view is significant only in extreme close-ups — which in any case need a reflex system.

As the subject distance changes, so does the angle of view covered on the film. The image field thus becomes smaller as the lens extension increases during focusing. The LEICA M finder compensates for that by including only the field of view at the nearest focusing distance, anyway. That is 0.7 m (28 in.) with the 28 mm to 50 mm lenses, 1 m (3¼ ft) with 70 to 90 mm and 1.5 m or 5 ft with the 135 mm lenses. Moreover, the field shown is that included within the 23 × 35 mm slide frame area and so also a little less than what goes into the full film frame. That way you never lose anything on the film that you saw within the appropriate finder frame.

With more distant subjects the film includes more than you see in the finder. In practice that is rarely a drawback, even with slides. With negative film it provides a safety margin — and you can always crop the print slightly. (Automatic photofinishing printers do so anyway.)

Sighting and viewing aids

With the projected bright-line frames the view convered does not change even if you look into the finder obliquely — at worst you don't see the whole finder area. In particular, to take in everything within the 28 mm frame you may have to squint to and fro behind the eyepiece. Fortunately such wide-angle views rarely need quick shooting and you get used to this style of viewing.

You also have to get used to the fact that the 28 mm lens intrudes into the bottom right-hand corner of the finder view. The same applies to the lens hoods of the 35 mm and 50 mm lenses. (But you can see enough of the bottom right corner of the view through the cut-outs in the hood.)

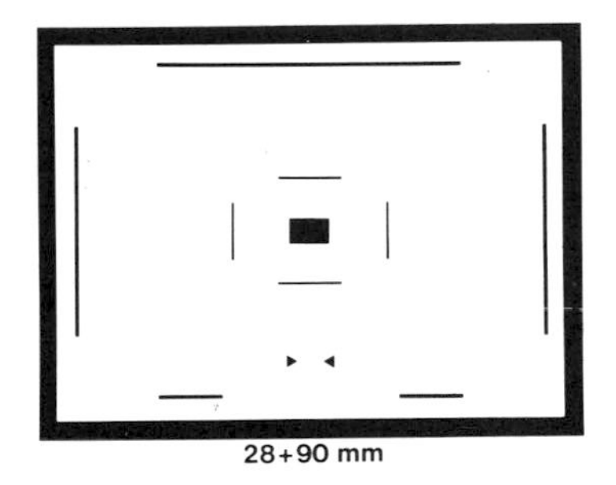

28+90 mm

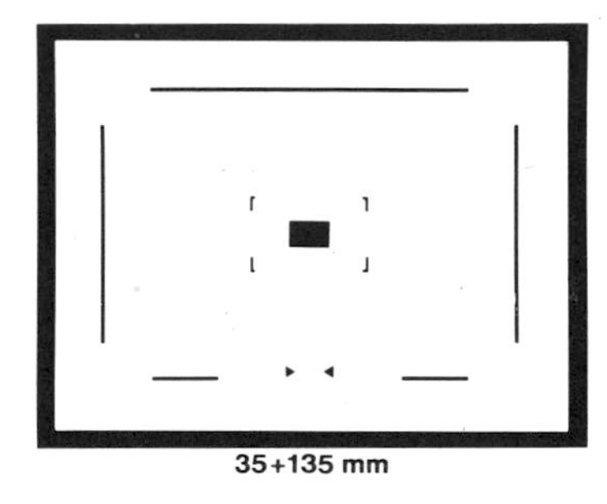

35+135 mm

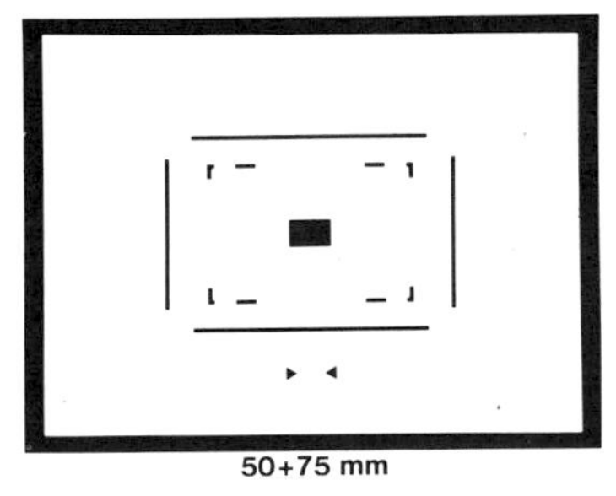

50+75 mm

Finder frames and signals in the LEICA M6. The frames appear in pairs according to the lens mounted or according to the position of the finder frame selector lever. The two inward-pointing arrow heads are the exposure monitoring LEDs; they light up together at a correct exposure setting.

One problem if you wear glasses is the short eye relief. The exit pupil is located very close behind the eyepiece. Glasses keep the eye a little farther behind the eyepiece, where you no longer see the whole field of the 28 or 35 mm lens. You may just manage with the 35 mm frame by squinting around in the eyepiece; the 28 m frame is hopeless with glasses.

Two ways out of this are either to use the separate 28 mm brilliant finder [12017 or 12007] or to mount eyesight correction lenses in the finder eyepiece. The brilliant finder fits in the hot shoe on top of the camera. You clearly see the whole view even with glasses, albeit at a rather reduced scale. A broken line in the top of the brilliant finder indicates the parallax-corrected upper frame limit at close range.

If you don't want to abandon the built-in finder, get correction lenses — available in powers from +3 to −3 diopters [14 061, 14 362 to 14 370] — and screw such a lens into the finder eyepiece. The eyepiece itself incorporates a −0.5 diopter correction which makes the finder image appear at a virtual viewing distance of 2 m — more comfortable than an image viewed at infinity. The effective range is therefore +2.5 to −3.5 diopters. Ophthalmologists may be able to provide lenses even beyond this range or to supply lenses with astigmatic correction. Leitz supplies empty mounts for such correction lenses.

One problem if you wear glasses and look through a finder fitted with a correction lens is that you have to take off the glasses or push them up to your forehead — and then put them on again for normal distance viewing. It might be a good idea to go with the camera to a specialist dealer who stocks the lenses and try viewing through the finder with and without correction.

The problem disappears with focal lengths of 50 mm and longer: with smaller bright-line frames you always see the whole field. On the other hand the 135 mm frame is rather too small; the 135 mm ELMARIT—M f/2.8 therefore has a finder attachment that enlarges the whole finder image 1.5 ×. The view now appears somewhat larger than natural size and both viewing and metering control are more precise.

The LEICA M3 finder differed from this scheme in showing a larger image scale but no frames for focal lengths shorter than 50 mm. The M3 needed special versions of 35 mm lenses with a finder attachment to reduce the viewfinder magnification (see THE EARLIER M SYSTEM chapter).

The rangefinder

The second part of the finder system is the optical rangefinder with its small rectangular area in the centre. This is a combined split-image and double-image rangefinder. If the lens is incorrectly focused, the central rangefinder field shows the subject with double outlines and low contrast. As you adjust the focusing ring on the lens, the double outlines fuse into one brilliant image. Thanks to the coupling between the rangefinder and the lens movement, this point of fusion is also the lens setting for a sharpest image on the film.

The rangefinder provides a split image, too: one of the outlines is displaced relative to the image surrounding the rangefinder area. Watch the upper or lower edge of the rangefinder field: the outlines become continuous across these edges at the same time as they fuse inside the rectangle.

Optical rangefinding relies on triangulation, i.e. on measuring the angle between the sightings of the object from two viewpoints. The viewpoints are the viewfinder and the rangefinder windows on the camera front; the distance between them is the rangefinder base length. On the LEICA M models this base length is just under 70 mm; the finder scale reduction brings the effective base length down to some 50 mm or 2 in. The base length determines rangefinding accuracy; in the LEICA M models this is greater than with almost any other 35 mm rangefinder camera.

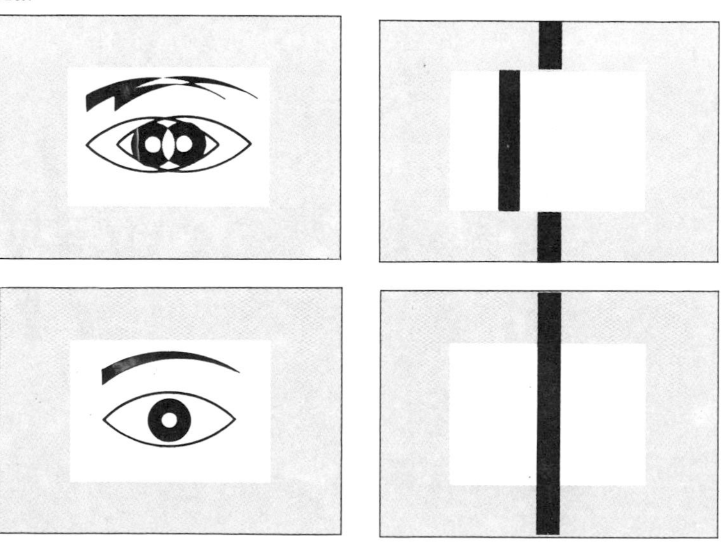

In its central rectangle the rangefinder shows both a double image and a split image with an outline displaced relative to the surrounding finder area. When the lens is correctly focused the double outlines fuse into one and become continuous across the boundaries of the rangefinder field.

The movement of a swivelling lens inside the rangefinder system, linked with the lens coupling lever, establishes the angle between the two rangefinder beams. Ranging accuracy also depends on the precision of these coupling elements — namely the roller on the coupling lever inside the camera mount and the cam surface the roller bears on in the rear of the lens. Keep these parts clean; preferably avoid touching them.

Rangefinder advantages and limitations

The fusion of the double image to one brilliant outline at the correct focus point is very clear. The rangefinder thus permits rapid and precise visual focusing even in poor light. It is in this respect superior to any reflex system, for optimum sharpness is not easy to judge on a dim screen image. Even the pure split image focusing aid in a reflex screen is less clear — and it works only at large lens apertures. Much of the fame of the LEICA and its popularity for action and feature photography derives from this fast and precise rangefinder focusing facility.

Rangefinder accuracy does not depend on the focal length of the lens but solely on the subject distance. With short focal lengths (21 to 35 mm) you can focus much more accurately by rangefinder than on any screen. With medium focal lengths (50 to 90 mm) rangefinder and screen focusing are reasonably matched for precision. Longer focal lengths require more accurate focusing than the rangefinder provides. The finder attachment of the 135 mm ELMARIT—M f/2.8 increases the effective rangefinder base length to around 75 mm for greater precision. With still longer lenses rangefinder focusing ceases to be adequate. Unless you are using a reflex housing, that is also the useful limit of the LEICA M lens range.

A second limitation is less serious: the double and split outlines in and across the rangefinder area are most obvious when they run at right angles to the base length. That means verticals with a horizontal camera hold. If you have to focus on prominent horizontals, do so with the camera held upright.

With the double-image rangefinder you can even focus on tiny bright detail in otherwise dark surroundings — for instance catchlights in the eyes of a portrait subject (equally easy with horizontal or upright shots). For our eyes are much better at detecting double and split images than the difference between absolutely sharp and nearly sharp. Double image fusion occurs abruptly at a slightest turn of the lens's focusing ring.

Finally, you can follow moving subjects faster in a double-image rangefinder — not just sports and action, but also children, animals etc. A useful way of focusing such subjects is to prefocus on a fixed point that the subject is likely to pass, then follow it in the rangefinder until the double images fuse into one. That is the point for releasing.

Exposure Technique

Light produces the image on the film. The latter records a range of colours and brightnesses according to the amount of light it receives. This light action depends on three factors: the subject brightness or luminance, the film's sensitivity or speed and the amount of light that gets through into the camera. The film speed setting of the LEICA M6 inputs film speed — according to the film loaded in the camera. The camera settings then control the amount of light required for a correct exposure with subjects of different brightness. These camera settings are the shutter speed for the duration and the aperture for the intensity of the light action. The two have parallel exposure effects but yield different pictorial results (see APERTURE AND SPEED COMBINATIONS.)

To find the correct exposure you have to measure the subject luminance. The built-in meter cell looks after that in the LEICA M6. Other M models (except for the M5) need an external exposure meter such as the LEICAmeter MR.

TTL metering of the M6

The first shutter blind of the LEICA M6 carries a white circular spot of 12 mm diameter. A silicon photodiode mounted inside the camera body points at this spot and there measures the average luminance of the image projected by the lens. The metering spot is located virtually in the film plane, the logical place for measuring image brightness and exposure. The LEICA M6 thus uses through-the-lens or TTL metering.

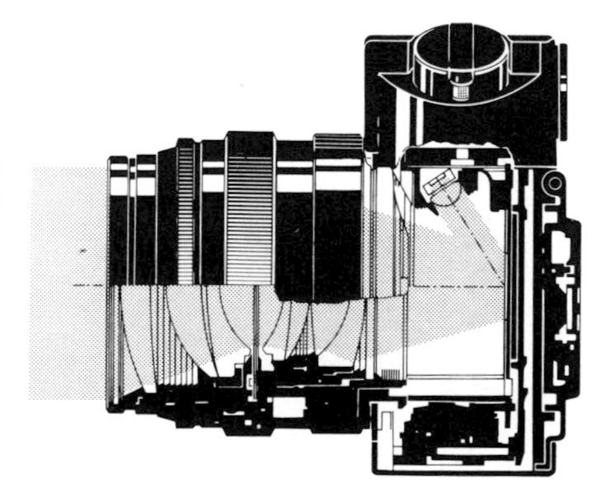

TTL metering in the LEICA M6: the silicon photodiode at the top inside the camera measures the luminance of the image projected onto the first shutter blind.

With this, exposure setting itself is supremely simple. Centre the main subject in the finder and slightly depress the release button. This makes one or two inward pointing red arrowhead LEDs light up in the finder — about level with the bottom line of the 35 mm bright-line finder frame. If the two LEDs appear equally bright, the exposure is correctly set. If only one LED lights, for instance the left one (pointing right), turn the lens aperture ring to the right — setting a larger aperture (lower f-number) — till the right LED lights up as well. If only the right LED lights, turn the aperture ring to the left to a smaller aperture (higher f-number). The direction of the LED arrow head is thus the direction in which you have to turn the aperture ring to reach a correct exposure setting.

In some positions both LEDs light up but one is brighter than the other. This means that the exposure is almost correct with half an f-stop underexposure (left LED brighter) or overexposure (right LED brighter). With only one LED lit the exposure setting is wrong by at least one f-stop or EV.

In daylight, with a film of ISO 200 and a preset shutter speed of $^{1}/_{125}$ sec, you should easily find an aperture setting to balance the LEDs within the lens's aperture range. If in very bright light the right-hand LED remains lit on its own even at the smallest lens aperture, set the shutter to a shorter time — between $^{1}/_{250}$ and $^{1}/_{1000}$ sec. If in poor light only the left LED lights at the largest lens aperture, set the shutter speed dial to a longer time — i.e. 60 ($^{1}/_{60}$ sec) up to 1 sec. (But support the camera firmly.)

To save battery power, the LEDs go out after about 10 sec. In that case slightly depress the release button once more. Also, the LEDs light only when the shutter is tensioned. (The white measuring spot on the first blind is not in position then either.)

Nor do the LEDs light at the B setting (time exposures) or when the lighting level drops below what the camera can measure. That metering limit depends on the lens speed; with an f/1.4 lens the lowest measurable luminance level in the subject is 0.25 cd/m^2. With an ISO 100 film that is equivalent to an exposure setting of 1 sec at f/1.4, or the slowest shutter speed setting anyway. You drop below the limit in still weaker light (or when you stop down the lens in poor light near the metering limit) so that less light reaches the metering spot on the shutter blind.

Finally, the left LED goes out when the lens cap is on the lens. So if no LED lights when all else seems OK, take that as a warning that you may have forgotten to remove the lens cap.

With lenses of smaller maximum aperture the low metering limit becomes higher −0.5 cd/m^2 with an f/2 lens or 1 cd^2 with f/2.8. With the 50 mm NOCTILUX f/1 the limit is lower at 0.13 cd/m^2.

The film speed setting in the camera back does not affect the metering limit, only the available exposure combinations. Thus with ISO 25 film, 1 sec at f/1.4 is the correct exposure for a subject luminance

The white metering spot in the centre of the first shutter blind covers about 13% of the image field for selective (large spot) readings.

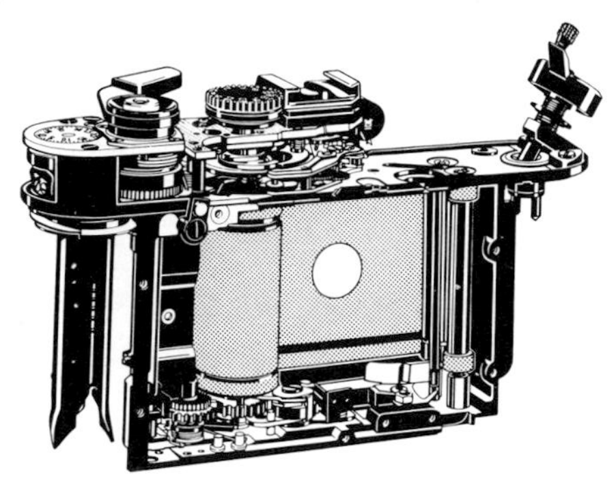

value of 1 cd/m^2 — still above the metering threshold. But if you turn the shutter dial beyond 1 sec to B, the LEDs go out — apart from the time exposures there is no way of setting a longer exposure than 1 sec. However, with a high-speed film of say ISO 800, 0.25 cd/m^2 needs an exposure of only $^1/_8$ sec at f/1.4. If a subject then needs ¼ sec, the LED again goes out.

There is also an upper metering limit determined by the smallest lens stop. With a 50 mm lens — which can stop down to f/16 — this corresponds to about 33 000 cd/m^2. With a still brighter subject the right LED would stay alight, but there is no way for the left LED to light as well, since there is no smaller aperture nor faster shutter speed. If the lens is capable of stopping down to say f/32 (e.g. the 135 mm ELMARIT f/2.8), the upper metering limit is — in theory — some 125 000 cd/m^2. But if the camera is not actually pointing at the sun, you rarely have to worry about upper metering limits: the average luminance of the brightest outdoor scene in brilliant summer sunlight rarely exceeds 8000 cd/m^2.

Spot readings

The 12 mm metering spot on the first shutter blind covers about 13% of the film image. Such a selective reading of a comparatively small image area often eliminates subject portions that could mislead the meter. The obvious example is the bright sky in a landscape. It equally applies to pictures of people (and other subjects) in front of a very light background) white wall, snow, etc). An average luminance reading of the whole image would here respond excessively to the very bright areas and cause underexposure of the main subject.

If that subject is significantly lighter than its surroundings (portraits against a dark background), the uneven brightness distribution taken in by average meter readings could similarly lead to overexposure of the subject itself.

In practice such special cases cover only about 10% of the subjects you would normally meet — it's not a thing to keep constantly in mind. So for set-ups of reasonably normal brightness distribution preset a shutter speed (e.g. 1/125 sec), aim at the subject, slightly press the release button and adjust the lens aperture ring unit both LED arrow heads light up equally brightly.

With scenes of unbalanced distribution (not the same as very high or very low overall lighting level — it's the job of the meter to allow for that) select a subject portion of medium tone and aim the camera to get that tone into the finder centre within the metering area (see below). Then set the exposure specifically for this subject part. (If such a metering area is to be outside the centre of the picture, set the exposure as before but reframe the view before exposing.)

The metering area

The finder does not show the extent of the metering area on the film. That would need different markings for lenses of different focal length — and would hopelessly confuse the existing finder frame markings.

Leitz recommends estimating the metering area as surrounding the rangefinder field with a circle whose diameter is about two-thirds the height of the finder frame for the lens in use. In area that covers about 23%, not 13% of the field within the finder frame. This is because — as mentioned — the finder frames cover less than the film.

Estimating this two-thirds diameter can be approximate; it is however a bother. Here is a simpler way. With any lens use the finder frame selector to show the frame of a 50% longer focal length. The metering area is then a circle of approximately this finder frame height. For instance when using a 35 mm lens switch to the 50 mm finder frame and imagine the metering area as a circle filling the height of the 50 mm rectangle. In the same way the 135 mm frame just contains the metering area for the 90 mm lens and the 75 mm frame for the 50 mm lens. (The latter two frames appear together, which makes switching frames unnecessary.)

With the 135 mm lens the metering area can be taken as a circle circumscribed around the rangefinder field. with the 21 mm lens (which needs a special finder) imagine the metering circle as contained within the 35 mm finder frame. However, there is no good match for the metering spots with the 28 mm and the 75 mm lenses, so there fall back on the two-thirds rule.

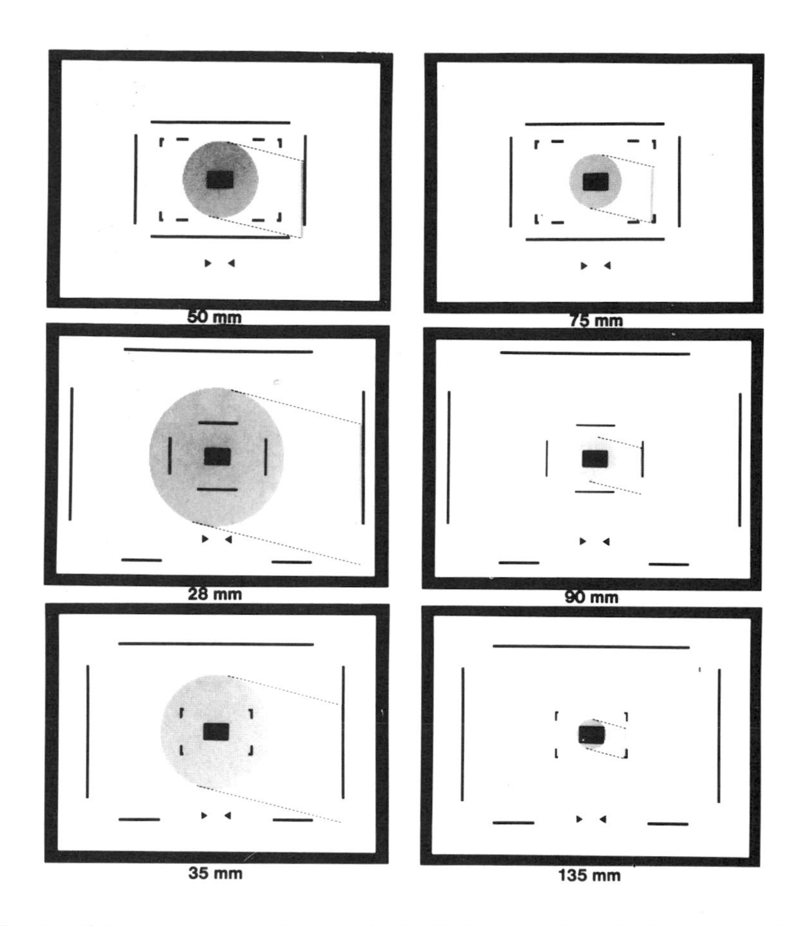

The size of the exposure metering area in the finder depends on the focal length of the lens as the finder magnification is constant and only the finder frames cover a larger or smaller area. Basically the measuring area covered by the meter cell is a circle with a diameter about two-thirds the height of the finder frame for the lens fitted on the camera. (That is more than 13%, as the finder frames take in less than the image actually recorded on the film.)

Lens restrictions

TTL metering with the LEICA M6 works with all currently available LEICA M lenses. With certain older lenses the rear lens tube protrudes further into the camera body and obstructs the measuring light path between the cell and the metering spot on the shutter blind. These lenses do not permit TTL metering — the LEDs simply fail to light.

The lenses involved are:

- The oldest version of the 28 mm ELMARIT—M f/2.8 with serial numbers below 2 314 920 (produced between 1965 and 1971);
- The 21 mm Super-Angulon-M f/3.4 and f/4.
- The 15 mm Hologon f/8.

Exposure compensation

Spot readings as described above, or the measuring of significant subject portions in scenes of unbalanced brightness distribution, usually yield correctly exposed negatives or slides without further ado. But a few cases call for special metering techniques or exposure corrections.

Very contrasty scenes where both highlight and shadow detail are important. Read important lightest and darkest areas separately, then use a mean value for the exposure. If for instance the highlight reading (brightest subject area) indicates f/16 and a shadow reading on a dark area f/4, this is a difference of four f-stops. The mean would be two f-stops from each end, i.e. f/8. (All these values assume a constant shutter speed). Still more constrasty subjects (more than 5 f-stops difference) rarely reproduce well in prints, though you may get away with it on slide film. So either fill in deep shadows with flash (see **Flash** in the EXTENDED SCOPE chapter) or select a right exposure for the main subject and sacrifice perfect rendering for the extremes of the range.

Subjects of predominantly light tones. If there is no mid-tone that you can conveniently read, even a spot reading leads to underexposure. So increase the exposure indicated by 1 to 1½ f-stops (larger lens aperture) — especially with slide film.

Subjects of predominantly dark tones. These need the opposite treatment to avoid overexposure: reduce the metered exposure by 1 f-stop.

In both these cases it is the predominant subject tones that count, not the general lighting level. Scenes in poor light need no correction — exposure measurement automatically allows for the lighting level. But a subject of mainly dark tones appears too light in the picture without such corrections; and underexposed snow can easily look like soot.

If you shoot such scenes with a wide-angle or normal lens, here is how you can make spot readings even more precise. Switch to a long-focus lens, measure the subject portions within the reduced measuring angle and set the exposure accordingly, then switch back to the shorter focal length for the picture itself. But you need some leisure for such antics.

Extreme low contrast. Landscapes in the rain and other dull-weather subjects are rendered rather dark on a slide film. So overexpose by half to one f-stop to bring out the mood without burying the image in impenetrable gloom.

Sunsets, night shots etc. For direct sunsets read the sky right next to the sun but don't include the sun itself in the metering area. That usually yields an optimum compromise between some foreground detail and a just-visible disc of the sun in the sky. If you measure the foreground, the sun becomes indistinguishable against the sky; if you read the sun itself, everything else becomes too dark. Try bracketing with a series of exposures at different settings and select the one you like best. Similar considerations apply to night scenes, especially with street lighting and large dark areas. When exposure times run into several seconds, increase the exposure by a further 100% to 400%, for at very low lighting levels the film behaves as if it had dropped in effective speed. Apart from that, different exposures yield a different balance between night and light and it becomes a matter of taste which combination you prefer.

The LEICAmeter MR

The LEICA M4-P has no built-in exposure meter; you can however couple it with an external LEICAmeter MR. The same applies to the other M models (M4-2, M4, M3, M2 and M1) except for the M5.

The meter cell of the LEICAmeter MR is a cadmium sulphide photoresistor. When mounted on the camera, the MR covers approximately the field of view taken in by a 90 mm lens. With a standard 50 mm lens an MR reading is thus slightly more selective (but not as precisely outlined) than the LEICA M6's TTL measurement. As the angle of view of the 35 mm to 21 mm lenses is larger still, readings with the constant acceptance angle of the LEICAmeter MR become particularly selective. With focal lengths of 75 and 90 mm the LEICAmeter yields virtually an average full-area reading and with the 136 mm lenses the meter angle is larger than the lens's angle of view.

In practice MR readings are slower and more cumbersome. To measure selected subject areas you have to go closer to the subject for the meter rfeading and then go back to the original viewpoint for the exposure. apart from that, special exposure corrections required are much the same as with TTL readings of the LEICA M6.

Handling is more complicated, too. First turn the milled setting wheel (next to the foot in the base of the LEICAmeter) to line up the white index mark on the wheel (black on chrome finished versions) with the B mark on the meter body. Depress the wheel and continue turning it as far as you can in the direction of the arrow. Set the shutter speed dial on the camera to B. Push the LEICAmeter — with the cell facing forward — fully into the flash shoe (accessory shoe) on the camera top, then turn the setting wheel back to line up its index with the B mark again. The stud in the underside of the wheel should as this point engage a notch in the shutter speed dial — between the settings for ½ and ¼ sec. Turning the meter setting wheel now also turns the camera's shutter speed dial and a large scale wheel on the top of the meter. The meter is thus coupled with the camera. (The M6 lacks — and of course does not need — the coupling notch in the shutter speed dial).

The scale dial on the meter consists of two sections: a lower dial carrying shutter speed and film speed scales, and an upper dial with two aperture scales and film speed windows. Set the film speed on the meter by rotating the upper dial to line up the film's arithmetic ISO rating opposite the index in one of the two ASA windows.

For a meter reading point the camera with the meter at the subject as described before and push the sliding switch on top of the meter to the left, then let go. Look down on the meter scales from above: the meter needle will have moved to one of the black or white scale divisions. (Letting go of the switch locks the meter needle position.) Now either:

(a) Preset a shutter speed — e.g. 1/125 sec — and read off the aperture value opposite the needle position. Set this aperture on the lens.

or:—

(b) Turn the meter setting wheel until the aperture you want to use (and have preset on the lens) lines up opposite the meter needle position. This at the same time sets the shutter to the correct speed.

The LEICAmeter MR has two measuring ranges, selected by turning a small button on the top. For the bright light turn the button with its arrow mark to the white dot; for poor light turn it to the red dot. Then read off the apertures accordingly on a white or red scale. (On bright chrome LEICAmeter models the bright-light scale and setting index are engraved in black).

If the meter needle hardly moves in the bright-light setting, switch to the red low-light range; if the needle runs past the end of the red aperture scale, switch to the bright-light range.

When you reach B with the setting wheel, you can raise the latter and continue turning. (This disengages the wheel from the shutter speed dial as for mounting the meter on the camera.) The exposure time scale now shows whole seconds up to 120 (2 minutes); these are time exposures at the B setting. The lowest metering limit is about the same as for the built-in TTL meter of the LEICA M6 with an f/2 lens — i.e. 0.5 cd/m^2.

A type PX 625 mercury battery powers the LEICAmeter MR. This button cell fits in a small compartment underneath, accessible on removing the meter from the camera. There is also a battery test switch: to use it push the black sliding switch on the front of the meter towards the rectangular meter cell window. This should make the meter needle move at least to the silver dot on the meter scale.

Using the MR meter

1. **Needle release button.** Pressing this button in arrow direction for about two seconds releases the indicator needle to measure the light level. When you release the button, the needle automatically locks in place, indicating the illumination "read" by the meter.
2 **Measuring-range selector switch.** For measurements in bright light, switch to the black dot; in poor light, use the red dot. When measuring outdoors in daylight, always switch to the black dot.
3. **Light window** with optics for the photo resistor. This controls the picture area measured by the exposure meter. It is equal to the field of the 90 mm viewfinder frame of the LEICA M cameras.
4. **Battery-testing switch.** To test the battery (Mallory PX 625), slide this switch (4) as far as it will go in the direction of the light-window (3). The needle (2) must then line up with the white battery-testing dot visible in the black area below the needle (11). If this is not the case, you must install a new battery.

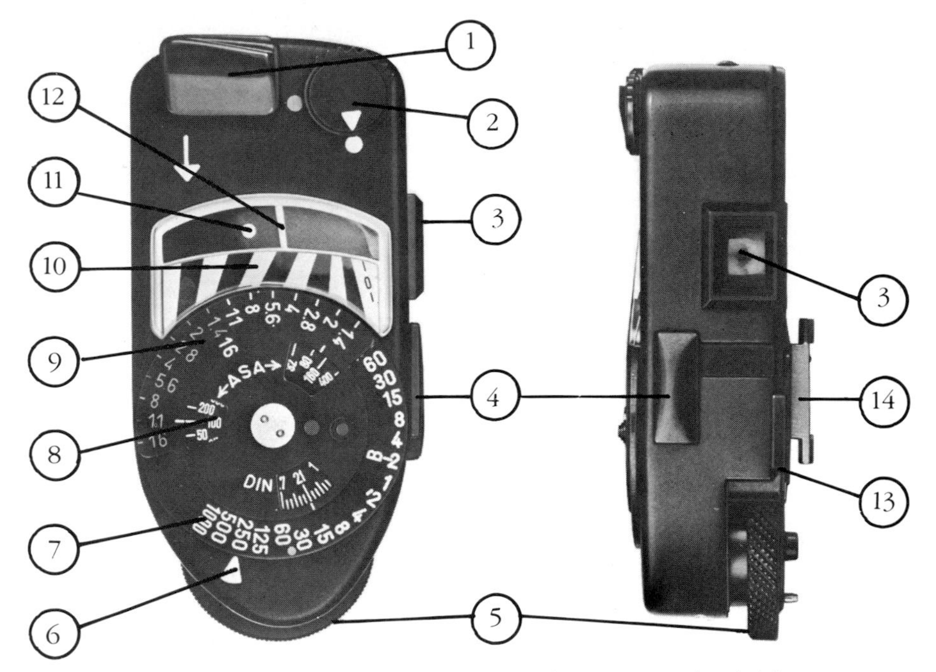

5. **Knurled knob** with coupling pin, the setting wheel. This serves to rotate the scales (7) and (9) and, when coupled with the LEICA, sets the shutter speed on the camera.
6. **Black triangle** for indicating shutter speeds.
7. **Time scale** for shutter speeds of $^1/_{1000}$ sec. to 120 secs.
8. **Film speed scale** for setting the film speed in ASA or DIN.
9. **Lens aperture scale:** white for high and red for low intensity according to the setting of the measuring-range selector switch (2).
10. **Channel scale** with alternating black and silver channels from which you can read off the correct aperture setting with one glance.
11. **Battery-testing spot** [see (4)].
12. **Indicator needle.** The needle is released by pressing the needle release button (1) in arrow direction. It locks in position when you remove your finger from the button.
13. **Battery housing lid.** Set the shutter speed dial to a value between two and four seconds. You can then swing out the lid by turning it in the direction of the arrow.
14. **Accessory foot** to attach meter to the accessory shoe of the LEICA M cameras.

With subjects of extreme contrast, as in these examples, you have to decide whether to match the exposure to the lighter or darker parts of the subject. Alternatively you could have used fill-in flash — but that would completely spoil the mood of these pictures.
Photo: Dr M. Beisert.

Aperture and speed combinations

As indicated, the exposure depends on two camera settings: (1) the aperture that controls the intensity of the light coming through the lens, and (2) the shutter speed that controls how long the light is allowed to act on the film. A large lens aperture combined with a short exposure time (fast shutter speed) can thus transmit the same amount of light to the film as a smaller lens opening with a longer exposure time. For instance $^{1}/_{1000}$ sec at f/2 is in exposure terms equivalent to $^{1}/_{500}$ sec at f/2.8 or to $^{1}/_{125}$ sec at f/4 — or to $^{1}/_{15}$ sec at f/16. Often such equivalent combinations are expressed in terms of an exposure value (EV) — all the above aperture/time pairs are equivalent to EV 12.

Sharpness factors

As a matter of fact, both the aperture setting and the shutter speed affect image sharpness. But they do so in completely different ways.

Shutter speed is directly linked with movement blur. Any camera movement while the shutter opens, especially during a longer exposure time, blurs the image on the film. Hence the recommendations of $^{1}/_{125}$ sec for hand-held shots. But subject movement, unless arrested by a sufficiently short exposure time, also causes image blur on the film. The faster the shutter speed (the shorter the time), the sharper a moving object appears in the picture.

In practice compromises are inevitable. For instance you may want to use a given aperture to secure sufficient depth of field (see below), with which the fastest shutter speeds would not provide sufficient exposure.

To eliminate movement blur we have to define limiting shutter speeds — exposure times that are sufficiently short so that the image of a moving subject does not appear visibly unsharp even in a reasonably big enlargement. The image movement that has to be arrested depends on the scale of reproduction (subject distance and focal length of the lens used) and on how fast the subject is moving. The limiting shutter speed required for this may be calculated or derived from more or less complex tables.

A simpler way is a rule of thumb. With a 50 mm lens, a subject 50 m away and moving at 50 km/h, a shutter speed of $^{1}/_{125}$ sec would yield a sufficiently sharp image. That is the limit — the exposure can be shorter but it should not be longer. It applies to movement at right angles to the camera direction (camera axis).

You can now derive limiting shutter speeds for other conditions from this 'triple fifty' rule. Thus a longer-focus lens would need a shorter

Dusk and night scenes offer particularly attractive, if subtle, colour effects. As the film effectively loses speed at lighting levels requiring long exposure times, increase the measured exposure by ½ to 1 f-stop. *Photo: Dr M. Beisert.*

exposure time to arrest the same movement — around $^1/_{500}$ sec with 90 mm — while with the 28 mm lens you could get away with $^1/_{125}$ sec. (For intermediate focal lengths use the next faster speed — e.g. $^1/_{1000}$ sec with 135 mm — or put up with slightly more movement blur at the next slower speed.)

Faster or slower movement involves analogous correction. Other factors being equal, you can arrest something moving at 25 km/h with $^1/_{125}$ sec. If on the other hand you go nearer, you need a faster speed, for instance $^1/_{500}$ sec at 25 m. (Nearer distance — like a longer focal length — magnifies the image and hence its movement on the film.) If the object moves obliquely towards the camera, you can again double the limiting time ($^1/_{125}$ instead of $^1/_{250}$), double it once more (to $^1/_{60}$) for movement directly approaching, or receding from, the camera.

Focal length also affects camera shake. If you only just manage to avoid camera shake at $^1/_{125}$ sec with the 50 mm lens, you should take hand-held shots with the 90 mm lens at least at $^1/_{250}$ sec.

You can set up and memorise similar ready rules for specific subjects — for instance 17/135/1000 for football shots (17 m distance, 135 mm lens, $^1/_{1000}$ sec), assuming the arms and legs of a running player to move at roughly 25 km/h. Of course 17m is not meant to be an exact value, rather a range between 15 and 20 m. Or a mnemonic for general movement in feet and miles: 50/50/15/500 for a 50 mm lens, 50 ft subject distance, 15 mph speed and $^1/_{500}$ sec exposure.

Aperture and depth of field

The lens aperture can control sharpness distribution. The aim of rangefinder focusing is to set the lens so that it yields the sharpest possible picture of an object at the focused distance. However if something at 5 m is absolutely sharp on the film, a part of the subject 4.99 m away won't suddenly be unsharp. Definition drops gradually in front of, and behind, the focused point. The image becomes noticeably unsharp only for objects outside a given distance range — the depth of field zone.

The lens aperture directly controls the extent of this zone. The sharp zone is limited with large lens apertures and grows as you stop down the lens. With a 50 mm lens focused at 5 m, the sharp zone at an f/2.8 aperture setting extends from about 4.2 to a little over 6 m (or from some 13½ to 19 ft when you focus on 15 ft). But at f/11 everything is sharp from as near as 3 m to nearly 20 m — or from 10 ft to 60 ft. The depth of field also depends on the focal length of the lens (the shorter the focal length the greater the depth) and on the distance (greater at far distances than at near ones).

You can calculate depth of field from mathematical equations or look up zones of sharpness in tables. Far handier is the depth of field indicator marked on every lens. It consists of pairs of white lines to each side of the focusing index — the triangular marker opposite the distance scale. F-numbers identify matching line pairs.

At a given aperture and distance setting the depth of field zone extends from the distance (on the distance scale) opposite the left index of that aperture to the distance opposite the right index for the same f-number. Thus with the standard lens set to 5 m or 15 ft as above, the left f/2.8 index (unmarked — there is not enough space for all f-numbers on the depth indicator) points to between 3 m and 5 m (very roughly 13 ft) on the distance scale, the matching right f/2.8 index to an estimated 6 m or 20 ft. The depth index lines for f/16 mark about 2.5 m at the left and infinity (the sign) at the right — at this setting everything is sharp from 2.5 m or about 8 ft to infinity.

Conversely, the depth of field indicator yields aperture and distance settings for a required sharp zone. To get everything sharp between 2 m and 5 m, turn the focusing mount with the distance scale so that the markings for 2 m and 5 m are opposite matching depth of field indexes. That is the case with the 50 mm lens when 2 m on the scale is opposite the left f/11 depth index and 5 m opposite the right f/11 line. That at the same time brings a distance just below 3 m or 10 ft opposite the focusing index — the required lens setting for this sharp zone. You then have only to stop down to f/11.

You often have to imagine intermediate settings. Note that the distance scale expands at nearer distances. Thus 20 ft is nearer to 25 ft than to 15 ft and halfway between 10 and 15 ft you are at a little over 13 ft. These depth zones are in any case only a rough guide to what would appear noticeably unsharp in the picture. As that is to some extent a matter of subjective judgement, these approximate indications are adequate for all practical purposes.

The rangefinder of the LEICA M2 and later M3 models also has a quick visual depth of field check in terms of permissible non-fusion of the double images (see THE EARLIER M SYSTEM chapter).

Pictorial unsharpness

So much for depth of field geometry. What of its application — what should be sharp or unsharp?

Our eyes constantly scan the view in front of us to convey a subjective impression of all over sharpness. In fact the depth of field of the eye is very restricted not only optically but also psychologically: as soon as we look at anything, we are visually aware of just that object. Everything else disappears from our field of sharpness and attention.

Such concentration on a main subject is a major pictorial technique. By deliberately restricting depth of field you can get very selective sharpness in the picture. For an extreme degree of such differential focusing go really close to the subject and use the largest available aperture. The depth of field indicator again shows the approximate zone covered; the further such unwanted detail is outside the depth zone markings the more blurred they will appear in the picture.

You can enhance this differential effect by using a longer-focus lens and going further away from the subject if necessary. Again expose at the largest available aperture — likely to be a problem only with high-speed film in bright daylight. With a medium-speed material of ISO 100 an average outdoor subject easily allows the use of f/2.8 at 1/1000 sec.

The other aspect of depth of field is the classical one of getting a great deal sharp in the picture, say people in the foreground together with an extended view behind. There is no problem if the light is good enough; just stop down the lens. If that is not feasible, the approach depends on the subject:—

(a) If it is the people or other foreground objects that matter, the background can be less sharp. So focus on the foreground and use as large an aperture as the light demands.
(b) If the foreground just provides human interest (scenics with figures) but must be sharp together with the background, go further away from the nearest item you want sharp, or use a wide-angle lens. Both ways yield sufficient depth of field even at a medium aperture.
(c) You may really need maximum depth from very near to fairly far, for instance large interiors with everything required sharp from 3 to 30 ft. Here use the smallest lens stop — possibly with a wide-angle lens — and put up with the long exposure time which that entails. (Remember to mount the camera on a stand.)

Creative movement blur

Before we leave the technique of sharpness, a few more points about movement. While movement blur is rarely desirable, it can occasionally reinforce pictorial impact. Take a child waiting at the edge of the road with traffic rushing past. Expose the stationary child at 1/30 sec and you enhance the impression of the busy rush around it.

There are other ways deliberately using movement blur. For instance swing the camera to follow a moving object and keep it centred in the finder while you expose at a fairly slow shutter speed. The object then appears sharp against a laterally blurred background — cars on a race track are a classic case. (But with racehorses you have to accept blurred legs — they move much faster than the whole animal.)

You can also use slower shutter speeds by catching movement at a 'dead point' — for instance a highjumper at the top of his or her leap. Be sure to release at the right moment, and possibly anticipate that a little. But with the rangefinder LEICA the delay between pressing the release and exposing is shorter than with a single-lens reflex where a mirror has to swing out of the way first.

The impression of sharpness also depends on the subject itself. A solid shape, for instance a jumbo airliner just rising from the runway, needs a fair degree of blur before it really looks unsharp. Yet much slighter blurring can be disturbing in distinct detail — say fine writing on the side of a passing van or truck.

The same applies to focusing unsharpness. An almost detail-less outline of a building in mist or fog does not have to be pinsharp. Brightly lit architectural texture does. In all cases pictorial unsharpness is a means to an end and should be a deliberate effect, not a byproduct of sloppy technique.

Exposure compromise

Before you take all this in deadly earnest, however, remember that while photochemistry, exposure, geometric optics etc are aspects of science, making pictures is an art. Also that art includes finding the best compromise between what you want and what you can achieve.

Here are some of those compromises.

First, the choice of different aperture/shutter speed combinations. No problem at medium lighting levels, equivalent to EVs between 8 and 15, but alternatives become restricted at the ends of the scale. Thus $^1/_{1000}$ sec at f/16 is usually the only combination possible at EV 18 — there is no way of selecting a faster speed with a larger aperture nor a slower one with a smaller stop. Similarly, with the f/1.4 lens 1 sec at F1.4 is the only available combination for EV 1. So either accept what these exposures involve in terms of depth of field and subject movement, or sacrifice the correct exposure.

Secondly, correct exposure is not as strict as it sounds. Most films can stand some under- or overexposure without completely spoiling the shot. This exposure latitude however depends on the film and also on subject conditions.

Colour print films (negative emulsions) can handle very little underexposure, perhaps half an f-stop or EV step, but easily 2—3 f-stops or EV steps of overexposure. With current colour print films in fact, grain gets finer (though not acutance) in an overexposed negative. With black-and-white films somewhat more underexposure is acceptable (if you are prepared to sacrifice some shadow detail) as in 1—2 EV of overexposure. Much more than that however makes the negative grainier and less sharp.

Colour slide films can stand some underexposure (up to 1 f-stop) but very little overexposure which quickly destroys highlight detail.

Exposure latitude increases, especially with negative films, for subjects of low brightness range. As mentioned, these may need about one f-stop extra exposure on colour slide film.

We view colour prints and colour slides under different conditions. Thus they cope differently with the brightness range of the subject. In

a colour print (also in a black-and-white one) the lightest and darkest image tones depend on the maximum and minimum light the print can reflect. In practice this tone range of a paper print is around 20:1 and rarely reaches 30:1. On the other hand the tone range of a colour slide depends on relative light transmission and can thus easily reach 200:1. A paper print therefore compresses the tone range of an original subject of great brightness range — the result looks rather flat. Slides can reproduce greater luminance differences in the subject. That is why projected slides look so much more impressive and why fastidious photographers prefer to shoot on slide film.

It follows that colour prints made from slides, especially of contrasty or brilliant subjects, tend to be disappointing. If you want prints from slides, choose subjects of more restricted brightness range (with neither very deep shadows nor too brilliant highlights), preferebly exposed by fairly diffused light.

Once you are tempted by the attractions of black-and-white photography you will sooner or later also develop and enlarge your own pictures. You can often enhance the pictorial impact of black-and-white shots by creative darkroom manipulation.

Photos: Hans Weinberger.

The Lens Range

Cameras used lenses of interchangeable focal lengths over a hundred years ago — when photographers often assembled their outfits more or less from scratch.. The LEICA however was the first 35 mm miniature camera to realise the idea of a transportable set of interchangeable lenses. Today the assortment is smaller than it used to be and therefore literally portable.

With a set of interchangeable lenses you can control the angle of view and image scale by alternative focal lengths, and perspective with different combinations of subject distance and lens. The two vital characteristics are the focal length and the angle of view.

In the camera the focal length of the lens controls the scale (as of course does the subject distance) at which a subject appears on the film. If the head of a person 6—7 ft away appears 5 mm high on the film with a 50 mm lens, the 90 mm lens projects the same head from the same viewpoint 9 mm high. With the 35 mm lens you would get a 3.5 mm head, and with the ultrawide-angle 21 mm just over 2 mm. If you want the head 9 mm high with the 50 mm lens you have to come closer, to say 3½ ft. So, changing lenses saves some legwork in the first place.

When an object appears smaller in the picture at a given distance, there is more space around it. A shorter focal length can thus cover a larger angle of view on the film format. (But the lens must be designed as a wide-angle lens, too.)

With our eyes we take in a horizontal angle of view of some 70° — or almost 140° if we count the total sweep of both eyes (without moving the head). Compared with that, the standard 50 mm lens on the LEICA covers about 39° horizontally. This rather blinkered view is regarded as normal for a 35 mm camera — another tradition established by Oskar Barnack and his optical collaborators.

To include in a picture what you can take in with both eyes — say the breadth of rolling hills and mountains, or the height of city skyscrapers looking above you, you need a wide-angle lens. For the these cover focal lengths from 21 to 35 mm, and horizontal angles from nearly 80° to 54° — quite a good range.

Longer focal lengths from 75 mm to 135 mm cover horizontal angles from 26° down to 15°. Image scales, relative to 50 mm, range from 1.5× to 2.7×, compared with the wide-angle scales of 0.7× down to 0.42×.

Wide-angle practice

Wide-angle lenses are useful whenever you cannot move back sufficiently from a subject to include all of it with the standard lens.

As such wide-angle shots take in what we cover visually by only scanning over the view, the picture ought to be viewed at a distance at which the eyes are again obliged to scan across the image from side to side. There are two practical ways of doing that: either to make a really big enlargement and look at it from close up, or to project slides on to a large screen and again watch from very near. This way — for instance with a 50 mm lens on a 35 mm slide projector — resembles wide-screen movie projection. So does the impact of the pictures.

This of course means looking at wide-angle pictures from much closer that we would normally do. At the viewing distance usual for a normal shot the wide-angle image appears unnaturally compressed and distorted in perspective To a large extent the reputation for perspective distortion of wide-angle lenses is due to the fact that the extended view covers more in depth, too, from far to very near.

Thanks to this exaggeration, interiors of small spaces photographed with extreme wide-angle lenses (e.g. 21 mm) appear greatly expanded. That's how a tiny boat cabin can look like a stateroom in a charter brochure. The camera doesn't lie, but it is very good at deceiving — and the advertising world makes extensive use of that.

Another kink of wide-angle distortion is geometric. People's heads and faces look egg-shaped when they appear at the edges (and especially corners) of wide-angle picture. This is pronounced with the 21 mm lens but visible even with 28 mm. So it is preferable to keep such familiar shapes away from the corners and edges of the view. (But deliberate distortion of this kind can also provide considerable pictorial impact.)

Perspective

The closer you approach an object with the LEICA, the larger it becomes in the picture. Take a tree, 20 ft tall and 30 ft away. The standard 50 mm lens projects it on the film a little under 1¼ in. — about 30 mm — high. A further tree 60 ft away would appear only 15 mm high. With the 21 mm lens the relative image heights would be 12.6 and 6.3 mm, and with one of the 90 mm lenses 54 mm (i.e. no longer all in the frame) and 27 mm. But from the same viewpoint the size relationship of the two trees remains constant irrespective of the actual image sizes.

Let's move back to 90 ft from the first tree. The standard 50 mm lens now projects it only 10 mm high on the film. But the second tree — still 30 ft behind the first one — is no longer twice as far away but only one-third further. Its image on the film is now 7.5 mm high, three-quarters (not half) as high as that of the first one. The 135 mm lens would show the trees 27 mm and about 20 mm high respectively — again in the same proportion. with this lens the first tree looks almost as big on the film as from 30 ft with the 50 mm lens. *But the second tree has become much bigger!*

These are the size relationships that control perspective in an image. The more various items that are nearer and further away differ in scale, the more perspective appears enhanced, and the greater the impression of depth in the view. The nearer you go to a subject extending in depth, the more exaggerated this depth becomes. That applies as much to trees (or a whole avenue) as to portraits. From close up, nearest parts such as the nose and chin appear overlarge compared with the ears or the neck. The effect may not be attractive, but in terms of geometric optics it is perfectly correct.

Perspective is determined exclusively by the camera viewpoint. The scale of reproduction however depends on the lens. Usually it is a combination of the two that controls the pictorial effect. By going close you can thus separate the foreground from the middle distance and background to emphasise the effect of depth in a shot. But you would have to reduce the image scale again — and take in what you lost of the view - with a shorter focal length (i.e. a wide-angle lens). This holds not only for broad landscapes. For instance an automobile in a near wide-angle picture may look like a dashing sports car. But when taken with a tele lens from further away it becomes a modest family saloon. (That's familiar ground to motor publicity.)

So to render facial proportions correctly in a portrait, keep your distance (at least 7—10 ft) and make the face appear larger with a longer-focus lens.

For perspective alone you don't even need the longer focal length. Enlarge the centre of the view taken from the same viewpoint with a shorter focal length: the perspective rendering is identical. But the more highly enlarged print loses some quality — it may appear more grainy and slightly less sharp. The alternative image scales and coverage of the various lenses make the most of the small film area every time.

Telephoto perspective is the exact opposite of wide-angle perspective: it compresses depth and distance. That is the familiar binoculars effect — not perhaps quite so dramatic with the relative 2.7× magnification of the 135 mm lens, but you can enhance it in a bigger print.

The main application of the LEICA long-focus lenses is the more distant close-up — pictures of people, children, animals etc at medium distances. That means a room length away, not long-distance telephotography. The latter needs much longer focal lengths which can be used on the LEICA M cameras only with a reflex viewing attachment (VISOFLEX). In rationalising its equipment range, Leitz allocated these applications to the LEICA R reflex models; they are no longer ideal fields for a rangefinder camera.

The M lenses

The table on page 168 lists comparative data for the various LEICA M lenses. Here are some more general explanations to complement that table's footnotes and remarks:

The angle of view is in theory the angle that the image subtends on the film but in practice the angle covered in the subject space. In their literature lens makers usually quote diagonal angles of view — which look more impressive with wide-angle lenses. As the side-to-side coverage (across the film frame) is more relevant to normal picture taking, the table lists horizontal angles as well as diagonal ones.

These angles are based on the 24 × 36 mm film gate size. The opening of standard slide frames (about 23 × 35 mm) and negative carrier masks in enlargers slightly reduces the angles.

The focal lengths quoted are nominal values. Standards specifications permit variations up to + − 5%, so a 50 mm lens could be anywhere between 48 and 52 mm. Most LEICA lenses of 60 mm and over carry a coding for the actual focal length — two digits at the end of the distance scale, just beyond the ft/m marking. They are the last two digits of the focal length value in tenths of a mm. Thus '13' on a 50 mm lens signifies an actual focal length of 51.3 mm, while '55' on a 135 mm lens stands for 135.5 mm.

The angles of view in the table refer to the nominal focal length and are rounded off (there is little point in being more precise than the permissible tolerances).

Configuration (number of lens elements and groups, i.e. assemblies of elements cemented together) is today far less important than a generation ago when the level of optical correction tended to be equated with the amount of glass in a lens. For optimum correction extreme wide-angle and extreme-speed lenses need more elements than longer focal lengths or more moderate maximum apertures. All lenses are coated, i.e. the glass/air interfaces carry special ultra-thin layers that absorb parasitic reflections and improve light transmission as well as image contrast.

Like other lens producers, Leitz from time to time updates designs and may replace existing lenses by more compact or otherwise improved versions. Order codes are changed only with more fundamental modifications. The table data refer to the latest versions (1986).

The near limit is the nearest distance setting on the lens, measured from the subject to the film place (marked under the winding lever on the top cover). The scale indicated (as 1:xx reduction) is the largest reproduction scale at the near limit; this depends also on the focal length. It is rather small and wide angle lenses as the focusing range is restricted to the near limit to which the coupled rangefinder can focus.

Lens hoods are normally supplied with current lenses; the order code refers to the correct type needed for possible replacement. (Older lens hood versions of different codes may also fit.)

Long tele lenses to be used with the VISOFLEX are also listed in the table but described in more detail in a separate chapter FURTHER LENSES.

Lens names fifty years ago used to designate special designs. As lens makers ran out of names for their innumerable new models and types, they largely ceased to bother with distinctive names. In the Leitz range (except for the TELYT models) the name now usually designates lens speed. Thus everything called ELMAR is f/3.5 or f/4, all ELMARIT systems are f/2.8, SUMMICRONS are f/2, SUMMILUX f/1.4 and NOCTILUX f/1or f/1.2. Since about 1978 the -M appendix identifies lenses for the rangefinder LEICA M models and -R for the SLR LEICA R range. Finally, -V (formerly also -M) are lenses usable only with the VISOFLEX reflex housing.

The wide-angle lenses

These cover three focal lengths — 35 mm, 28 mm and 21 mm — of different applications.

The 35 mm lenses (SUMMILUX-M f/1.4 and SUMMICRON-M f/2) are really extended standard lenses. Some photographers use them routinely in place of the 50 mm lens. The angle of view is 40% wider and the object area taken in about double that of the 50 mm lens — which is useful for landscapes and features or when shooting in crowds. Indoors the wider angle also helps to cope with cramped space problems. (Popular compance miniature camera often have a fixed 35 mm lens.) It halps equally (by allowing greater aiming errors) if you want to shoot unobtrusively from the hip, i.e. without raising the LEICA to the eye. Finally, the wider angle is useful for informal groups, especially indoors. (But a larger camera is better for formal group photography.) The 35 mm lens suitable for single portraits. To get the head reasonably large in the picture you have to go close — which exaggerates perspective unfavourably. (On the other hand the 21 mm lens is better for cartoon-like distortion effects.)

The choice of lens speed (between the f/2 SUMMICRON and f/1.4 SUMMILUX) is largely a matter of what you are prepared to pay. The extra f-stop in speed of the SUMMILUX may be useful in very poor light; professionals are anxious to have every possible reserve in speed. In the other hand the nearer focusing limit of the SUMMICRON-M (0.7 m instead of 1 m) is also an advantage.

The 28 mm ELMARIT-M f/2.8 is the ideal lens for all-round wide-angle pictures. Compared with the standard lens, the angle of view is over 60% larger, which distinctly expands the coverage without too much risk of the kind of wide-angle distortion mentioned earlier. Perspective enhancement remains within acceptible limits, too. Older LEICA models — other than M6 and M4-P — need a separate accessory finder [12 017 or 12 007] with this lens and switching between that brilliant finder and the LEICAmeter MR is awkward. Older versions (pre-1971) of the lens have a rear section protruding by about 16—17 mm which interferes with TTL measurement in the LEICA M6 (and M5). On the current models this rear section protrudes no more than 11mm.

The 21 mm ELMARIT-f/2.8 is the extreme wide-angled lens for really exaggerated perspective effects. Pictorially this can be very effective but also calls for certain precautions in handling. In the first place, hold the camera pointing straight, neither up nor down, as the extended angle of view also exaggerates the effect of any tilt, i.e. converging verticals. To avoid geometric wide-angle distortion keep not only faces but also other familiar shapes away from the corners of the field. For instance a round table located there below camera level is liable to spread to a ludicrous oval or egg shape. This is quite a problem in architectural interiors — for which the focal length is otherwise very useful (especially in confined spaces).

Latest version of the 21 mm ELMARIT-M f/2.8 — an ultrawide-angle system covering a horizontal angle of almost 80°.

The wide-angle coverage increases of course vertically as well as horizontally, and with the camera held level that can include a lot of uninteresting foreground. If necessary, crop away that unwanted area during enlarging — even if that yields a long panorama-type strip. The same applies to upright shots. When the verticle angle becomes 81° and, without tilting the camera up, easily covers high buildings from quite nearby.

All LEICA M models need the brilliant finder [12 012 or 12 002] supplied with this lens; fit it in the camera's accessory/flash shoe.

Standard lens speeds

Why three 50 mm lenses? They are spaced one f-stop each apart in speed (and quite appreciably in price), but the choice may often be more a matter of prestige than utility. for with current film speeds and the vast majority of subjects you are likely to cover with the standard lens, f/2 is fully adequate. For the professional LEICA user the extra f-stop of the SUMMILUX-M may well be worth the extra cost over the SUMMICRON-M; but with the NOCTILUX-M you pay a great deal for the additional speed. So that is a special lens for perhaps press and feature photographers who constantly have to shoot without flash and in poorest light.

The 50mm SUMMICRON-M f/2 has one advantage over the other two 50 mm lenses as a universal lens: it focuses down to 0.7 m or some 28 in. (largest scale 1:11.5), against 1 m or 3 ¼ ft for the others. The current version [11 819] of the 50 mm SUMMICRON-M is also the lightest and most compact standard lens produced for the LEICA M it weighs 195 g and protrudes just 42 mm.

The 50 mm SUMMILUX-M f/1.4 weighs almost twice as much as the SUMMICRON-M (it contains larger and heavier glass elements) but is only a few mm longer and fatter. At its nearest setting this high-speed standard lens yelds a 1:17 scale — not a strong point for close-ups.

Lens settings on the 50 mm SUMMILUX-M f/1.4. The aperture ring at the front engages at full and half f-stop intervals. The wide ribbed ring below it is the focusing mount with the distance scale (in both feet and metres). The depth of field indicator nearest to the camera body shows that at this setting of 10 m, or 30 ft, an aperture setting of, say, f/8 would render sharply everything from 15 ft, or just under 5 m, to infinity. The tiny figure '14' marked sideways next to the 'm' mark on the distance scale encodes the exact actual focal length of the lens — in this case 51.4 mm.

The 50 mm NOCTILUX f/1 weighs more still at 580 g — more than the LEICA M6 body. A special characteristic for poor-weather and night photography is maximum optical correction to elimate flare and coma. This greatly reduces the risk of stray light and irradiation from bright light sources (e.g. street lamps) in the picture. With the NOCTILUX such sources appear as fairly sharp point images even at the edges of the picture and not as irregular blurred spots (coma). In the NOCTILUX, coma correction received priority over optimum resolution. Thanks to minimum stray light the image looks very sharp, but the SUMMICRON-M resolves finer detail. In night photography freedom from flare and coma is more important than maximum resolution — an example of how optical design compromises may allow for the intended application of a lens.

At the full aperture of the NOCTILUX depth of field is very limited, so precise focusing is vital. (At 6 ft the sharp zone is under 4 in. deep.) But that again is less of a problem in night and similar subjects with extended dark and shadow areas lacking in detail.

The tele lenses

To bring distant detail nearer with longer focal lengths it is logical to aim at double or triple the scale of reproduction. The focal lengths of 90 and 135 mm follow this rule approximately (exactly if you assume 45 mm to be a standard focal length). Hence 90 mm is the most useful second lens after the standard one. As it forces you to back away a little from the portrait sitters, perspective gets better. At 5 ft — normal conversation distance — this lens reasonably fills the frame with a head-and-shoulders view. With it you concentrate on the subject, eliminate unwanted near foreground and also restrict depth of field.

The last point applies strictly only when comparing sharp zones at equal subject distances. You may for instance enlarge a shot taken with the 50 mm lens to make the main subject as big in the print as from a negative taken with the 90 mm lens. The sharp zone in this latter print will appear visibly shallower. But what is sharp there will look sharper than in the 50 mm shot because the latter was enlarged more. On the other hand if you use the 90 mm lens to make the image scale larger, instead going closer with the 50 mm lens, the depth of field (at a given aperture) in front of and behind a nearish subject depends mainly on the image scale. In other words, the actual sharp zone is as deep at 15 ft with the 90 mm lens as at 8½ ft with the 50 mm lens (which yields the same image scale) — namely around 18 in. in total at f/2.8. At greater distances — more than say 100 focal lengths — the shorter focal length yeilds greater relative depth of field.

The 135 mm lens enhances all this still more: at 5 ft a head really fills the frame.

The more recent 75 mm SUMMILUX-M f/1.4 falls somewhat between the stools of the above scale comparison. It is again a lens for professional feature and similar assignments to make the most of available light conditions — for instance at indoor sports events. In size and appearance it resembles the 90 mm SUMMICRON-M f/2 — often a better compromise of weight and image scale for such jobs.

One advantage of the 90 and 135 mm lenses is their larger image scale at the near limit of 1 or 1.5 m respectively — 1:9 in both cases. Hence an object about as wide as a LEICA camera would fill half the width of the image frame. It's not a large close-up but quite useful for many medium small items. Incidentally, 90 mm is also the ideal focal length for close-ups with the VISOFLEX (see the FURTHER LENSES chapter).

The 75 mm SUMMILUX-M f/1.4 is at 625 g the second-heaviest lens directly usable on the LEICA M cameras. But the camera with this lens is comfortable to hold. Grip the lens with the left hand, setting the aperture and focus on the two closely spaced rings. In view of the more limited depth of field the index lines of the scale show only very approximate values and spread out (as on all longer-focus lenses). At f/1.4 depth is negligible. A lens hood is built-in.

Longer-focus high-speed lenses: the 75 mm SUMMILUX-M f/1.4 (left) and the 90 mm SUMMICRON-M f/2 (right).

A wide-angle lens, in this case 21 mm, particularly effectively emphasises near-to-far depth of a scene. *Dr M. Beisert.*

The 90 mm SUMMICRON-M f/2 resembles the 75 mm lens in shape, size and control layout but offers a more versatile combination of speed and image scale. The single f/2 index on the depth scale again signals negligible depth of field at this aperture.

The 90 mm Tele-ELMARIT-M f/2.8 is a full f-stop slower than the 90 mm SUMMICRON-M but far lighter and more compact. It protrudes just 20 mm more in front of the camera than the 50 mm SUMMICRON-M.

The 135 mm ELMARIT-M f/2.8 is the longest and heaviest of the LEICA M lenses; the weight inludes the 1.5 × finder attachment. When mounted on a LEICA M camera the attachment magnifies the finder image and with it the rangefinder field and base length. Leitz designers considered the attachment essential for more accurate focusing to cope with the limited depth of field at the full aperture. The lens hood again extends.

The longest lens normally suitable for rangefinder focusing is 135 mm. the ELMARIT-M f/2.8 of that focal length has a built-on finder attachment that magnifies the rangefinder image for more precise focusing. (Here shown on a LEICA M2.)

The 135 mm Tele-ELMAR-M f/4 is by today's standards quite slow but much more compact than the 135 mm ELMARIT-M. For most outdoor subjects (where you are more likely to need this focal length) f/4 is

Composition of colour and shapes. You may need a longer focal length to concentrate on essential elements in a closely cropped image. *Photo: Dr M. Beisert.*

however adequate.

The lens unit itself of both 135 mm lenses unscrews from the focusing barrel; you can then mount it (with suitable adapters and a helical focusing mount) on the VISOFLEX for close-up photography. See the FURTHER LENSES chapter for more details of this and other combinations with the VISOFLEX.

Lens hood arguments

To see better when looking into the sun you usually shield your eyes with your hand. A lens hood similarly enables the lens to see clearer. It does so especially when bright lights not actually in the picture shine directly at the lens — e.g. the sun, but also powerful lamps in low-light situations. (What counts is the intensity of the source relative to the general lighting level.)

According to photo books you should use a lens hood for every exposure. True, but a bother. So if you have the leisure, it's worth fitting the hood. Professional feature photographers rarely get round to it.

Present-day lens coating, especially multicoating, largely limits one problem that a lens hood is supposed to cure, namely scattered light within the lens which reduces image contrast on the film. Such light flare becomes particularly troublesome when, say, the sun is actually within the lens's field of view. But there no lens hood helps, either. It's also true that all stray light kept off the film improves image quality. So by all means use a lens hood when you can — but not at the cost of missing a picture.

Some lenses have an extending hood — pull it forward when needed and push it back when you put the camera away. The lenses concerned are the current version [11 815] of the 75 mm SUMMILUX-M (but not the earlier [11 814] model with push-on hood), the 90 mm SUMMICRON-M [11 136 and and earlier 11 829] and the 135 mm ELMARIT-M [11 123].

Push-on hoods are supplied with the other lenses. A tubular hood [12 575] fits the 90 mm Tele-ELMARIT-M and 135 mm Tele-ELMAR-M. Press the two keys at the sides of the hood, push onto the lens to engage the groove around the front and let go of the keys. When not in use you can reverse the hood on the lens and fit a special lens cap [14 033] over the end. There is also a screw-in rubber hood for the 90 mm f/2.8; push it back over the lens when not required.

The lens hoods of the 50m mm (and shorter-focus) lenses protrude into the bright-line frames in the finder. For some of these the hood has cut out rear sections: turn the hood to view the bottom right ocrner of the subject field through one of these cut-outs. These hoods for the 50 mm and 35 mm SUMMICRON-M (except for the earliest model of

Such feature stories are particularly easy with the LEICA M6 as the photographer can remain unobtrusively in the background. *Photo: Heldur J. Netocny.*

the latter) are the versions [12 538] or [12 585]; you can again reverse them on the lens and use a special lens cap. Similar hoods for the 50 mm and 35 mm SUMMILUX-M are the models [12 586] and [12 504] respectively. A special feature of the latter is that the front section unscrews to take Series 7 filters (50.8 mm or 2 in. in diameter), for the 35 mm SUMMILUX-M is the only current LEICA M lens without a screw thread for filter.

To reduce vignetting (corner shading) with the 28 mm and 21 mm lenses, their hoods — very short, anyway — are rectangular. A locating stud on the lens front ensures correct mounting. The hoods for the current [11 804] 28 mm and 21 mm ELMARIT-M are the types [12 536] and [12 537] respectively. the [12 501] hood for the previous 28 m ELMARIT-M [11 801] is similar and also fits the odler 21 mm Super-Angulon-M f/3.4 [11 103].

Finally, the 50 mm NOCTILUX-M [11 821] takes a bayonet-mounted lens hood [12 619], similar to that for the first version of the 75 mm SUMMILUX-M [lens hood 12 539].

Filters

If the spectral composition of the prevailing light does not suit the film in use, you can modify the light with filters. These also alter the colour effect in the picture. Nowadays that largely arises with exposures on colour slide film if the light is too blue (subject lit by skylight only) or too reddish (evening sun or tungsten lighting). Filters are less important with colour negative film as colour casts get corrected in printing. But the use of correction filters while shooting can still improve the quality of prints produced in bulk on photofinishing printers.

This group covers a range of bluish and amber filters (from very pale up in each case), the former serving for colour correction when you expose daylight type colour slide film by tungsten lighting. Amber or orange filters range from colourless UV-absorbing (to eliminate blue cast due to ultraviolet rays in for instance alpine views) through the pale amber Skylight filter for warmer colour rendering to distinctly orange correction filters for tungsten type film used in daylight.

Apart from the above there are a few more types:

Filters for black-and-white film modify the way in which the film interprets colour hues as greys, especially to retain or create monochrome contrast between colours of similar luminosity. Thus a yellow filter darkens the rendering of blue sky in landscapes to make clouds stand out better. Orange and red filters enhance this effect. An example of colour contrast control would be a shot of red roses and green foliage which a normal black-and-white film renders in the same grey tones. With a green filter however the roses become darker against lighter foliage, with a red filter lighter against darker leaves.

Polarising filters absorb polarised light and — in suitable orientation

— suppress light reflections and glare from shiny surfaces. They can also darken the sky in colour pictures and have various special uses in scientific photography. To check the filter effect look at the subject through the filter and rotate the latter until the reflections appear weakest. Mount the filter on the lens in this position (without rotating it further). Polarising filters suppress glare only from reasonably transparent material surfaces — water, varnish, polish, plastics, glass and glazes etc — but not metals.

Finally, there are numerous filters for special effects on black-and-white and colour film. They include innumerable split, graduated, diffusing, scattering, star effect etc filters from specialised suppliers. Leitz's own filter range comprises polarising filters; yellow-green, orange, red and blue filters for black-and-white film; and UV-absorbing filters for colour slide film.

Filters usually screw into the front lens mount. Screw fittings are available in several standard sizes from 39 mm to 60 mm (even larger for certain TELYT lenses); the table (page 168) lists filter fittings of current lenses. Unfortunately the filter size is one parameter that tends to change with new versions of a lens. Older models of nominally the same lens (sometimes even with the same code No.) may sometimes need different filter sizes. If you have to buy a filter for such a lens, take the lens to a photo dealer and find the right filter size to fit on it.

So-called Series filters used to be fashionable at one time. Adapter rings held these unmounted filters in the lens thread. This was cumbersome and is now rarer, though with appropriate adapters you can still use certain Series filters on newer lenses. One exception is the 35 mm SUMMILUX-M f/1.4 which has no filter thread and therefore holds Series 7 filters in the lens hood.

Filter arguments

The use of filters also seems to be a fashion sponsored in part by makers of special effects filters. Filter effects are fine if you know what you want to achieve — but filters for their own sake are less advisable. Optically lenses are designed for optimum performance using the glasses in the lens. Additional unforeseen elements (including filters) tend to impair image quality. Pictures will be sharpest without a filter; preferably use the latter only when really necessary.

A further argument against getting too involved with filters is the wide range of filter sizes for LEICA lenses, the after effect of a lack (exceptional for Leitz) of product planning.

Filters absorb light; the picture therefore needs more exposure to compensate. TTL metering of the LEICA M6 (and M5) allows for this light loss and therefore needs no further correction. When measuring exposure externally with the LEICAmeter MR, increase the result by the filter factor quoted for the filter in question (i.e. use a larger lens aperture or slower shutter speed).

Independent lenses and filters

As the Leitz filter range is limited, it may be necessary to fall back on other filter makes — especially for Skylight and similar filters. Look for optical quality: preferably use plane-parallel dyed-in-the-mass glass filters by reputable filter manufacturers.

Special effects filters on the other hand are usually dyed plastic. Where the special effect counts — star patterns, multi-images etc — rather than top image, quality, such filters are adequate. But avoid plastic filters for precise recording.

There are also a few non-Leitz lenses that fit the LEICA M cameras, in particular those made for the Minolta CLE rangefinder camera. The latter is a development of the LEICA CL (made for Leitz by Minolta) and uses the same bayonet lens mount. However, do not use on the LEICA M the lenses specifically produced for the LEICA CL (the 40 mm SUMMICRON-M and 90 mm ELMAR-C f/4). You can physically attach them to the LEICA M cameras but because of a different cam matching system they do not couple accurately with the LEICA M rangefinder.

There are virtually no other lens makes fitting the LEICA M cameras; Leitz carefully guarded its patent rights over the M bayonet mount, assuring the maintenance of the high standards LEICA users expect.

Selecting an Outfit

Really you can take pictures with just the LEICA M camera body and one lens. However, that buys you only future potential; in shooting terms a single lens takes you little further than a considerably cheaper camera with permanently built-in lens.

The classical way of building up an outfit would be to buy the camera with the standard lens to start with, and then add further lenses as you can afford them. But it is more logical to plan an outfit from the outset. What you hope to get in the end should govern the initial purchase.

If you want to stay with a standard and a medium long-focus lens, choose 35 mm and 90 mm, i.e. without a 50 mm lens. This is a compact and adequate basic outfit for many purposes — and it fits in a small holdall case. As far as lens speed is concerned, the 35 mm f/2 SUMMICRON-M is good enough, especially with its nearer focusing limit of 0.7 m against 1 m with the 35 mm SUMMILUX-M. My choice for 90 mm would be the SUMMICRON-M f/2 — but the 90 mm Tele-ELMARIT-M does weigh only half as much.

If you are keen on wide-angle subjects, start with the 28 mm ELMARIT-M rather than 35 mm. The first longer focal length should still be 90 mm, but you will need 50 mm in between (which is why you should plan ahead before deciding to buy a 50 mm lens). On the other hand 35 mm can still count as an extended standard lens — but the angles of view (65° and 54° horizontally for 28 mm and 35 mm respectively) don't differ that much. Generally 28 mm is a good compromise between reasonable wide-angle coverage and not too much wide-angle distortion (see **Wide-angle practice** in the previous chapter).

What else? You will need a flash unit with at least 30—35 as a (metric) guide No., with contact foot and preferably tilting reflector, a bounce reflector (see **Which flash unit?**), a synch lead, table tripod with ball head (useful for close-ups and small objects), cable release, polarising filter for the 35 mm or 50 mm lens and possibly a Skylight filter.

Going further

A basic outfit with lenses from 35 or 28 to 90 mm can of course be extended in both directions. The 21 mm ELMARIT-M (with special wide-angle finder) is worth considering for ultrawide-angle work, but not as a substitute for 28 mm — even if you sometimes want the extreme 81° angle, you will more often need the more moderate 65° of the 28 mm lens. (A good compromise might be 24 mm — which at present does not figure in the LEICA M lens range.

At the other end, 135 mm again complements rather than replaces 90 mm. If you often need this focal length, the 135 mm ELMARIT-M is worth having. Despite the extra bulk and price the magnified rangefinder image is a real boon.

Then start looking at special equipment for specific requirements: extreme-speed lenses (75 mm SUMMILUX-M, NOCTILUX), the winder M and so on.

The ever unready case

If you go about with the camera ready to shoot, you are best off carrying it over one shoulder, possibly hidden under a jacket. When not actually using the camera, keep it reasonably protected. Camera makers (including Leitz) offer so-called ever-ready cases where you can in theory open the front and shoot without removing the camera from its case. Unfortunately, such cases are not particularly 'ready' in practice; they are not only bulky but outright uncomfortable for holding the camera steady.

A better way is a soft camera case (if you take the camera with just one lens) or a holdall equipment case for an outfit with several lenses and accessories. The soft case protects the camera — against knocks and scratches as well as against dust — yet you can quickly pull such a case off the camera and stuff it in your pocket. Leitz ever-ready cases are also removable (the strap is attached to the camera, not to the case) and provides more protection if you should drop the LEICA. But I find the soft case much more convenient.

Holdall cases

You can carry the camera on its own without a case and at a pinch an extra lens in your pocket. But once you have a second extra lens, you need a separate container of some kind. There is a wide range of universal and holdall cases available, from comparatively small ones for the camera body and a couple of lenses — to big outfit cases to hold a couple of cameras, numerous lenses, winder, flash, films and so on. Leitz has several alternatives in leather; there are also innumerable types in plastic, water-proofed nylon and other materials — and at all price levels.

The best way of buying such a case is to take your whole outfit to a photo dealer and try out different cases until you find one of the right size, quality and features. Waterproofed padded nylon cases with adjustable inside divisions are ideal, as you can then reorganise the space when your outfit grows. The most flexible types use Velcro-fixed dividers.

Other points to note:

- You should be able to dump the most frequently used camera combination (e.g. with standard lens and winder) in a compartment as it is, without dismantling.
- The same combination should also be instantly accessible, i.e. at the top when you open the case.
- The other items must be accessible, too. Deep cases are not too good if you have to remove a lens to get at your flash unit.
- The carrying strap must be tough (e.g. nylon webbing) and run right round the case underneath. A LEICA M outfit is rarely that heavy a load; but if you keep snatching up a full case, the strap fitting sooner or later gives way. It cannot do that if a continuous strap runs round the bottom. A wide strap (say 2 in.) makes the case more comfortable to carry.
- Avoid further containers (such as lens cases) in the holdall case itself. The purpose of the holdall is to hold everything for instant access, without wasting time wrapping or unwrapping items.
- One holdall case is not the last word on this subject. Start with a small case for a small outfit. When that gets bigger, get a second, bigger case. You can still pack the small one (for instance in your luggage on a trip abroad), so that you don't have to carry the big one all the time to go out with just the camera and a couple of lenses.
- The bag should also have one or more pockets for small items. Not just filters, lens hoods and film, but also a ball pen, a small notebook, waterproof felt pen (to write data on the film leader), a small blower brush to clean the lens, spare batteries for the camera and flash unit. I often also carry a micro-cassette recorder (for quick notes of subject details — more convenient than writing them down), a tiny battery tester for AA cells, a penlight torch and a piece of chamois leather for lens cleaning, kept in a plastic film can. These extras are of course a matter of individual choice.

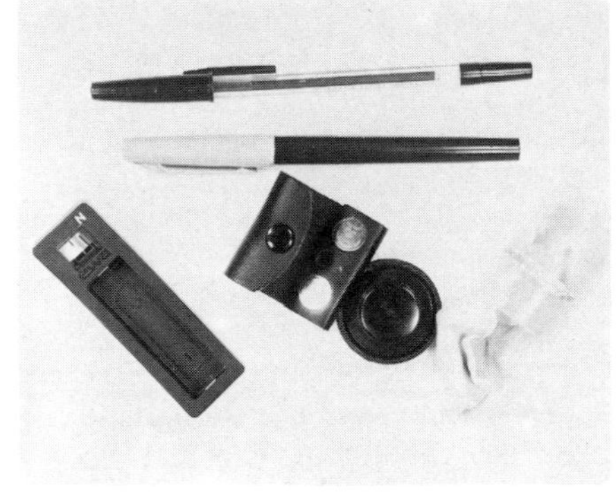

Small accessories in the holdall case. Useful items to carry are a ball pen, a waterproof felt pen (writes on plastics and film), spare silver oxide button cells (centre, for the LEICA M6 only), a battery tester for AA cells (used in flash units) and a small lens cleaning chamois leather (here in a plastic film box).

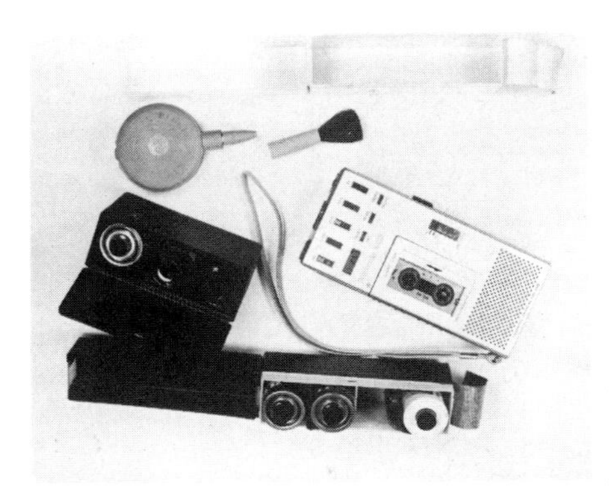

I also often take a micro-cassette recorder to record notes, a rubber blower brush for removing dust from lenses and camera, and several compact film containers holding 3—4 cartridges. (These I carry in my pocket to avoid X-raying at airport security checks.)

A second body?

Professional photographers are rarely happy with just one camera — they often carry a second camera body. True, a bit of a luxury, but very convenient, if you are using two kinds of film at the same time (say slide and negative material). The second camera body is then little more than a glorified alternative film holder. Apart from the LEICA M6, I have had an M4 for more than fifteen years; it is now a spare body. So if you have an earlier LEICA and switch to an M6, the old camera still remains a useful part of an outfit.

Extended Scope

Apart from lenses and small accessories, two other items are relevant to LEICA photography: the Winder M and flash units. The former is a Leitz accessory specifically for the LEICA M6, M4-P and M4-2. Flash on the other hand relies entirely on independent equipment.

The Winder M

From the outset sports and press photographers liked the 35 mm camera for its fast shooting ability of taking picture sequences. Motor drives came into being to speed up the shooting rate. Early ones included a clockwork motor drive for the LEICA some fifty years ago. Today's Winder M allows shooting at up to three pictures per second.

With the winder, remote control of the camera becomes feasible, too. A remote release alone is not enough, for you have to wind the film and retension the shutter after every exposure. The winder is useful for sports photography but also for sequences of people, photographic interviews and features. A motorised film advance distracts less from picture taking, and — unlike the machine-gun-like rattle of many SLR camera drives — the LEICA winder is comparatively unobtrusive.

Attaching to the camera

The winder consists of the motor unit and a battery case. Joined together the two make a unit 59 mm tall — the amount the winder adds to the camera height. The length exactly matches the camera; in depth the winder protrudes about 3 mm below the lens at the front and is flush with the body at the rear.

The base carries a tripod bush at one end and a screw with coin slot at the other, securing the battery case. The order code [14 402] is also marked in the base. This refers to the battery case; the code for the current winder version [14 401] is visible in the base plate on removing the battery case.

The top has virtually the same layout as the inside of the camera base plate, with base plate lock and take-up spool flange. Next to the latter is the motor drive shaft that engages the coupling dog in the camera. Instead of a fold-down key the lock uses a lever which at the left-hand camera end swings from its open position at the front right round to the back to secure the winder to the camera. This latter position, marked ON, also switches on the motor.

As the winder replaces the regular camera base plate, you can attach it only with the camera empty. To remove (or fit) the winder while the camera is loaded, you must switch it against the base plate in total darkness (or in a changing bag) — or unload the film and reload it again (see **Partly exposed films** in the FILM HANDLING chapter). But that is cumbersome.

The LEICA Winder M (here in its earlier M4-P designation) permits sequence shooting at up to three pictures/sec. It replaces the camera's regular base plate.

After loading the film in the normal way, check that the leader is correctly located in the take-up spool core, close the back and attach the winder in place of the regular base plate. The base plate lock of the winder must open (lever at the front at the left-hand camera end). Check that the winder is properly in position, then move the locking lever fully to the rear to ON. The motor engages, tensions the shutter and straightaway advances the film (if the shutter was released). Release, carefully tighten the rewind crank as described before, and release again. While the motor winds on, the rewind crank must turn anticlockwise to show that the film is advancing. Release once more: the film advances again (recheck on the rewind crank) and the frame counter moves to No. 1.

Single shots and sequences

The camera with winder is now ready to run. Every time you press the release, the winder advances the film immediately after the exposure. This works at any shutter speed; you can let go of the release even at the slower speeds as the winder can only advance the film once the shutter has closed. At the B setting for time exposures (where the winder is pointless) the shutter remains open as long as you keep the release depressed; the film again advances as soon as the shutter has closed.

For picture sequences press the release (at any setting other than B) and keep it gently depressed. With fresh batteries and a fast shutter speed the release and film advance now cycle at up to three exposures per second. You can also feel the mechanism alternately raising and releasing the button. That's why you should press gently; if the mechanism cannot raise the button, it cannot cycle, either.

The top of the winder has the same fittings as the inside of the camera base plate plus a drive shaft to engage the camera's transport coupling shaft (to the left of the film path diagram in the camera base). The lever at the right secures the winder to the camera.

To switch off the winder, push the locking lever from ON to the left against a mechanical stop. (As you closed the camera the lever moved past this stop; the latter prevents inadvertent opening of the camera.) Now release and wind the film as without the winder. If you switch on after an exposure, the winder advances the film; if you switch on after winding manually, the winder operates after the next exposure.

As the camera triggers the winder mechanically, any remote control must involve mechanical releasing of the camera. You can do that with an extra-long cable release (at best limited to about 6 ft), with a pneumatic release or an electric remote release. A pneumatic release uses plastic tubing with a rubber ball at one end to operate a cable release-type plunger pin at the other; this is effective up to about 30 ft but becomes uncertain in response much above that. Electric remove releases actuate a mechanical plunger, as on a cable release, attached to the camera release. The link can be a wire (up to perhaps 100 ft), an infra-red pulse (with suitable sending and receiving equipment) or a wireless signal.

Photo accessories manufacturers supply such devices through photo retailers.

For a remote-controlled exposure, mount the camera on a tripod, possibly together with a bracket or other fixing for the remote release device.

The combined locking lever and switch on the winder. Moved fully to the ON position it closes the motor circuit.

The battery case

Four AA size batteries in the batter case power the winder. Use either alkaline manganese cells or rechargeable nickel-cadmium accumulators (nicad cells) — see **Battery types.**

To change batteries remove the battery case from the motor base: unscrew the milled screw with a coin. (If not tightened too firmly you can even unscrew it with your fingers.) Pull off the case and swing open the inner cut-out retaining cover. Insert four cells in the compartments; note the + and – polarity markings. The two cell pairs must point in opposite directions.

Refit the battery case on the winder, pushing the contact end against the contact pins protruding next to the tripod bush and screwing in the retaining screw at the other end.

If you use the winder a lot, it may be worth taking a spare battery case [14 402] ready loaded with batteries. Tie a rubber band round it to stop the retaining cover from swinging open and spilling the batteries.

Unloading

When the film is finished, the winder whirrs briefly and stops. Swing the rewind clutch lever on the camera front to R (at this the winder completes a started cycle) and rewind the film normally as described in the

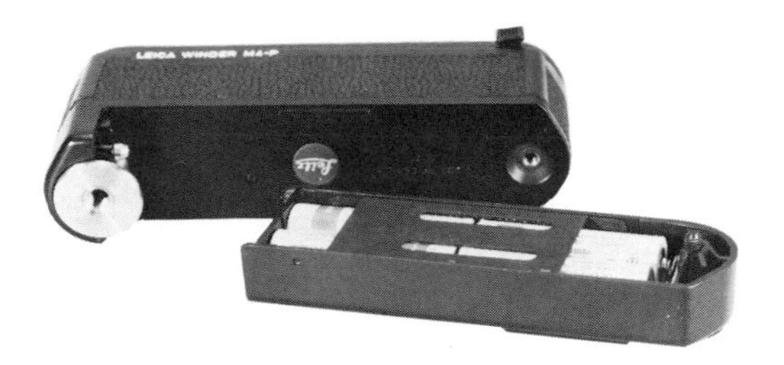

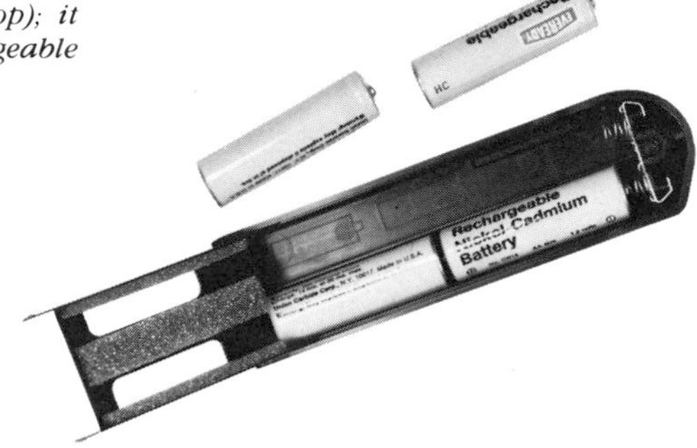

The battery case is removable (top); it takes four size AA cells (e.g. rechargeable nicads).

FILM HANDLING chapter. There is no risk of tearing the film, for the winder cuts out when the excess film tension is still well below the tearing strain of the film perforation. But don't press the release again after swinging the clutch lever to R — that would stress the film repeatedly.

To remove the winder push the locking lever to the left against its stop, raise the lever to move it past the stop and swing fully forward. Remove the winder like the regular camera base plate.

The M4-2 Winder

An earlier version of the winder [14 400; serial Nos. from 10 350] also fits the LEICA M6, M4-P and M4-2 cameras; models of the latter with serial Nos. below 1 502 001 need adaptation by Leitz.

The M4-2 Winder differs from the model M or M4-P (the Winder's earlier designation) only in the battery case design. The latter here extends across the whole of the winder base and is attached at one end with snap-in contacts. A milled screw with coin slot again secures it at the other end. On this model you can also connect the battery case [14 227] via a cable [14 229] and — to avoid losing battery performance in cold weather — keep the battery case in your pocket. The same cable permits the use of external power sources, e.g. larger battery sets for greater capacity in remote control applications.

A still older model [14 214] uses the same [14 227] battery case but has a pin protruding next to the drive shaft in the winder top. This pin, operated by a release coupling in the M4-2 camera, switches on the

The Winder M4-2 has a different battery case design that extends across the full length of the winder base.

motor after the exposure. The mechanism is more elaborate (and less reliable); this winder is not usable on the LEICA M4-P or M6 which do not have that special release coupling. Avoid this winder (recognised by the protruding pin), even if you see it second-hand.

How worth while is a winder?

Complete with batteries the Winder M weighs over 400 g, or some 14 oz, which is quite a lump to carry with the camera. It is useful mainly for fast sequencing; 2—3 frames/sec is beyond even the fastest manual operator. The convenience of motorisation in normal shooting is counterbalanced by the bulk and wieght. You are often better off winding manually, without this extra load.

On the other hand the camera hold with the winder is convenient. Rest the left end on the palm of the left hand; the left thumb, index and middle fingers then easily operate the lens aperture and focusing rings.

The winder and camera assembly stand well balanced on a table top, supported by the tripod bush plate at one end and two ridges (to line up flash brackets up to 20 mm wide) at the other. The lower centre of gravity helps the camera to stand firmly with standard or wide-angle lenses (but it becomes front-heavy with 75 mm and longer focal lengths).

Many interesting shots are missed on journeys and holidays because the photographer could not be bothered to carry a heavy SLR outfit. The compact LEICA M6 is an ideal camera to take travelling. *Photos: Dr M. Beisert.*

Comfit
ORANGE SQUASH
MIXED PICKLE
TIN FRUITS
FRUIT JUICES
TIN VEGETABLES

21

Flash

As a portable light source, flash is not only useful where the prevailing light is inadequate; it can equally light up shadows and reduce excessive brightness ranges in daylight subjects.

Flash shots are almost invariably synchronised — which the focal plane shutter in the LEICA permits only at shutter speeds of $^1/_{50}$ sec or slower. A lightning symbol on the shutter speed dial marks this shortest synch time.

So the basic rule for flash shots with the LEICA is never set shutter speeds faster than $^1/_{50}$ sec. Otherwise the flash fires while the shutter partly covers the film; generally part of the image is then missing in the picture or there is a disturbing boundary between the flash-lit and non-lit (underexposed) sections.

A synch contact built into the shutter closes the firing circuit of a flash connected either through the hot shoe in the camera top or the flash socket just below the shoe in the rear. The LEICA M4-P and earlier models have two such sockets; use the one marked with X or a lightning symbol. The second socket (marked with a bulb symbol or M) was provided for flash bulbs — now obsolete. On the LEICA M5, M4 and earlier models only the flash socket is usable as the shoe there has no built-in contact.

Flash outlets: the hot shoe with integral contact and immediately below a co-axial socket for synch leads. Both are X-synchronised for electronic flash.

To fit the flash unit either push it into the hot shoe or connect to the camera with a bracket (usually by screwing the latter into the tripod bush). In the latter case the electrical connection must in any case go through the flash socket in the back.

If the subject includes large white areas, increase the exposure for colour slide film by about ½ f-stop. The bottom picture is a typical case where a spot reading (on the foreground figures) cuts out the misleading effect of the surroundings.

Photo: Dr M. Beisert.

Which flash unit?

Various manufacturers offer countless flash units in innumerable versions.

Most amateur flashes are more or less compact units to fit the camera's hot shoe — which is the most convenient way of using the flash, though it does not necessarily yield the best lighting.

Here are a few guidelines for chooshing a unit from the large (and constantly changing) range on the market:

Automatic flash duration control. Preferably select an automatic or computer flash with a sensor that regulates the flash output according to the light reflected from the subject. Otherwise exposure control becomes complicated. The unit should have at least two output levels (aperture setting options in automatic mode); these apertures should be the same for all film speeds. That is, the flash should provide a greater operating range with the faster films, not compensate higher film speed by requiring a smaller aperture setting.

Guide number. Should be at least 30—35 (metres, ISO 100). Lower-power units may be adequate with fast films or for fill-in flash with near subjects but are otherwise too limited in application.

Lighting angle. The flash should at least cover the field taken in by the 35 mm lenses, about 55° horizontally. According to makers' specifications most flash units do so, but the light intensity in the corners may drop to half of what it is in the centre. That makes the angle of coverage look good on paper but is less useful for practical pictures. It's no problem if you photograph people or small groups largely centred in the view finder. If really even illumination is important, either take the picture with a longer-focus lens (at least 50 mm) or select a flash with a larger angle (indicated as 65°, for a 35 mm lens). On the other hand, spreading the light over a larger angle reduces its average intensity (and hence guide number). You can extend the angle with some flashes by placing a diffuser in front of the reflector. There are also soom reflectors adjustable to different lighting angles — useful for the LEICA, as a narrower angle setting increases the flash range and guide number.

Tilting reflector. The flash reflector should be able to tilt up (and possibly sideways, too) for bounce flash effects (see **Flash lighting**) — which all but the smallest current flashes do. A downward tilt of 5—10° is useful for close-ups, too.

Desirable is also a subflash for filling in with bounce flash — either a reflector system that beams part of the bounced flash forward again, or a second, permanently forward pointing, small flash tube and reflector.

Batteries. Most flash units use the same battery size as the winder — convenient as you have only to worry over one battery type (see below).

Small to medium-size flash units fit directly in the camera's flash shoe.

Displays. Calculator dials or slide rules in the rear of the unit usually show the film speed setting (must be set separately on the flash), power level, aperture to be used and available distance range in auto mode. Sometimes LEDs or liquid crystal displays (LCD) show these data more impressively and/or more readably. But the simpler indications are just as reliable.

Handle or grip type flashes. Large flash units (guide number of 35 and over) often become too heavy for the LEICA's hot shoe; the usual way is to attach them to the camera via a bracket. These are generally more professional press outfits, less matched to the intimate rangefinder LEICA style of photography. On the other hand the lighting effect is better if the flash is not mounted directly on the camera. Separate hand grips and brackets are available for smaller flash units of certain makes, too (e.g Metz, Osram, Vivitar) to turn them into handle types. The grip may hold further batteries to increase flash capacity. Link such units to the camera either via a synch lead plugged into the LEICA's flash socket or by an external sensor to fit into the hot shoe. That sensor maintains automatic exposure control when the flash is used off the camera for special effects.

Battery types

The Winder M and most small to medium-size flash units take size AA penlight cells (international designation LR6). Two types suitable for photographic use are disposable alkaline (or alkaline manganese) dry cells and rechargeable nicad accumulators. Both are available from numerous makers with similar (or different) type designations. Both have advantages and drawbacks. (Ignore ordinary zinc carbon cell torch batteries, except for emergencies — their capacity is too low and output too variable.)

Alkaline cells (e.g. Mn 1500, AM-3, Varta 4006, Eveready E 91 — to quote the commonest type codes) yield 1.5 volts per cell or 6 volts for a set of four. They are available everywhere and hence convenient. Nicads may cost four to eight times as much but can be recharged several hundred times — much more economical. For nicads you also have to buy a mains charger. Check that it is usable with different voltages that you might meet on trips abroad.

In either case take spare batteries (recharging nicads usually takes hours — say overnight).

Official specifications for alkaline batteries quote twice as high a capacity as for nicads. The latter have a more uniform output and fail only when fully exhausted (but then cut out completely). With alkaline batteries output drops gradually: the winder and flash units begin to recycle more slowly. Long flash recycling times are rarely acceptable; the practical capacity (while cell voltage is above 1.1 volts) is thus fairly similar for alkalines and for nicads.

Larger grip type units (and the supplementary hand grip of smaller units) sometimes take larger size C cells (LR-14, AM-2, Mn 1400 etc) — again available in alkaline and nicad versions. The capacity is about three times that of size AA cells.

Based on its own test conditions, Leitz quotes a capacity (at 20° C) or about 150 films of 36 exposures for a set of fresh alkaline or freshly recharged nicads in the Winder M. That sounds (and is) a lot, for the 50-milliamp micromotor in the winder is very efficient. As the batteries run low, the motor gets slower or — with nicads — cuts out abruptly.

Battery capacity for flash depends of course on the unit — the higher the guide number, the more current the unit uses. Impatient professionals whose time is worth a lot of money tend to discard flash batteries as soon as recycling slows down. (Such cells are still usable in low-load equipment, such as shavers or micro-cassette recorders.)

Remove alkaline batteries from a winder or flash unit that is not in use for a week or more (see CAMERA AND LENS CARE chapter).

Flash procedure

Here, then, is a summary of the special steps needed for flash exposures:

(1) Set the camera's shutter speed dial to the flash symbol ($^1/_{50}$ sec) or a longer time.

(2) Mount the flash unit in the camera shoe, or fit it with a flash bracket and plug in the synch lead. On the LEICA M4-P or earlier models plug the lead into the X socket (or the one marked with a lightning symbol), not the M (flashbulb symbol) socket.

(3) Set the film speed on the flash unit. Select an aperture suitable for the intended distance range and set it on the lens. If the flash permits several aperture options for a given distance, select the aperture according to depth of field requirements.

(4) Switch on the flash unit and check the ready signal lights.

(5) Sight the subject, focus and shoot.

In automatic or computer flash units a sensor responds to the flash light reflected back from the subject and controls the flash duration for a correct exposure. This assumes a right film speed setting on the flash unit and appropriately selected aperture on the lens. With some flash units a further auto check signal (a blinking LED or a beep) indicates whether the exposure was correct — i.e. whether the subject was within the distance range for automatic operation.

If you cannot manage with the indicated aperture and distance combination, switch to manual mode to use a larger aperture. This is useful if for instance you have loaded a high-speed film but the flash unit requires a small aperture for the fast film. Use the guide number for correct exposures in manual mode. Measure the subject distance (focus with the rangefinder and read off the distance — in metres — on the lens scale) and divide this into the guide number. The result is the f-number to which to set the lens. Keep the subject distance constant — in manual mode there is no automatic compensation for distance.

The aperture applies to average subject conditions, with some light reflected from walls (indoors). That light is absent out of doors, so here set the next larger aperture. (Automatic flash allows for that, too.)

Flash lighting

Flash shots are easy with the flash mounted on the camera. But the resulting flat front lighting — the typical newspaper flash effect — is not particularly attractive. Results often look better either with bounce flash or with flash off the camera.

For bounce flash tilt the reflector up so that it lights the ceiling and the latter bounces the light back as soft even illumination. You need of course a suitable ceiling — light, neutral in colour and not too high. The longer light path via the ceiling and the latter's diffusing action waste a lot of light — which is why the flash needs a guide number of at least 35 (metric) to get anywhere with bounce lighting. A sufficiently near wall can also bounce the light — provided that the flash reflector can swing sideways.

The sensor of an automatic flash should still point at the subject (not at the ceiling). Bounce flash is too uncertain without sensor control; correct exposure in manual mode is then largely a matter of luck.

If the ceiling is too high, attach a bounce reflector to the flash — a smaller reflecting screen fitted or held above the upward pointing flash to redirect the light forward again, but much more spread out.

While direct flash is harsh, bounce flash tends to the other extreme with excessive softness. some frontal fill-in light helps matters and there are flash units that automatically divert about 10% or so of the bounce lighting directly forward at the subject. A subflash (a small second flash tube in its own reflector) has the same effect.

Off-camera flash can yield more versatile effects (side, top, etc, lighting) and involves setting up the camera and flash (even several units) like lights in a studio. Synch leads link the camera with the flash units, or — better still — use a slave flash. This is a small flash unit on the camera, fired by the latter, so that the light triggers further flashes controlled by photocells. Correct exposure becomes more complicated in such set-ups; ideal is an external sensor to control the flash duration of all the flashes together. Failing that, use a special flash exposure meter.

Filling in shadows

Besides its traditional role as a portable light source, flash is becoming important for auxiliary lighting, too. It balances difficult illumination, for instance outdoors in the shade, under trees etc where faces of people and other detail tends to appear dark and flat. When you shoot into the light the shadows facing the camera are also very dark and benefit by being filled in with flash.

The aim with fill-in flash is to support, but not to compete with, the prevailing illumination — usually daylight. In practice that means that the flash intensity, i.e. the flash exposure, should at most amount to half the level of the existing ambient light. But the flash should also remain correctly synchronised with the LEICA. This is easiest with an automatic flash unit and the following procedure:

(1) Establish the required exposure for the subject areas lit by the prevailing light. For against-the-light pictures take spot readings of brightly lit subject parts, not the shadows.
(2) Set an appropriate aperture/speed combination for this exposure (see the EXPOSURE TECHNIQUE chapter) but with a shutter speed not faster than $^1/_{50}$ sec (lightning symbol on the shutter speed dial) or $^1/_{30}$ sec. Stop down the lens accordingly.
(3a) Either: set the flash unit to double the speed of the film in the camera and the aperture option selector to the aperture already set on the lens.
(3b) Or: with the film speed set normally set the aperture option or range on the flash unit to one f-stop larger (next lower f-number) than the aperture setting on the lens.
(4) Check that the subject is within the indicated distance range for automatic mode, then expose. The flash should now have filled in the shadows to a level a little below that of the main lighting for luminous natural result.

If the flash has no setting for a sufficiently low light output or small aperture, reduce the flash power by attaching a wide-angle diffuser (where available); this usually reduces the exposure by the equivalent of one f-stop. Or if there is no other way, tie a white pocket handkerchief (single layer thickness) over the flash reflector.

A normal full flash exposure — within the flash set to the same film speed and aperture as the camera — exposes the shadows normally and overpowers the prevailing daylight. The effect is not very natural but sometimes called for in press and feature photos which should never show faces in shadow. On the other hand you can restrict the fill-in effect further by setting the flash to 1½ or even 2 f-stops larger than the lens aperture. This more dramatic lighting is often effective in colour slides: on prints it tends to make shadows appear too dark.

In bad weather or with an overcast sky the flash can also stand in for the sun. Measure the exposure as for a normal daylight shot, and again set a combination with a shutter speed not faster than $^1/_{50}$ sec. Divide the resulting lens aperture into the guide number of the flash (in manual mode); the result is the required flash distance to simulate a sunlight effect. Set up the flash separately at this distance to light the subject from the required direction. If this calls for too long a synch lead, fit a small flash unit in the camera's hot shoe and use a slave cell to fire the main flash.

Matching the light colour is important with such combinations. Electronic flash and daylight (other than possibly late afternoon sunlight near sunset) should pose no problems. Prevailing tungsten light is however much too reddish to go with the flash. Depending on the film type and correction filter used, that gives either a correctly lamp-lit picture with bluish fill-in, or correct rendering in the filled-in areas but very reddish colours everywhere else. There is no easy way of getting over this — you have to make the best of it.

Further Lenses

The LEICA made its name as a rangefinder camera and not as a single-lens reflex. Yet over half a century ago a reflex housing turned the LEICA into the first 35 mm reflex system, logically extending the range of the rangefinder system. Later called VISOFLEX, these reflex housings remained part of the LEICA equipment range for nearly fifty years. The most recent VISOFLEX 3 model ran virtually unchanged for twenty years to the beginning of the 1980s and is still an interesting side avenue of the LEICA M system.

For the VISOFLEX made two applications — now assoicated with the LEICA R reflex system — accessible to the rangefinder LEICA: telephotography and large close-ups. If you intend to specialise in these fields, a true SLR such as the LEICA R4 is more convenient. But the VISOFLEX usefully complements the picture taking style of the LEICA M — even if handling it is rather more cumbersome, especially exposure metering with the LEICA M6. (That is what eventually — and regrettably — persuaded Leitz to stop producing the VISOFLEX.

The VISOFLEX 3

The housing functions as an extension tube with an optical register (distance between front and rear bayonet flanges) of 41 mm. A hinged mirror in this space redirects the image formed by the lens to a ground glass screen in the top.

For the exposure a release lever swings up the mirror and then presses on the camera release button. You observe the screen image via a removable focusing magnifier. Alternatively, a prism finder turns the assembly of the LEICA M with VISOFLEX into a single-lens reflex, though without the automatic refinements of present-day SLRs. A tripod bush in the base of the VISOFLEX balances the combination on a tripod (with less strain than in the camera's tripod bush).

The VISOFLEX 3 with 65 mm ELMAR f/3.5 lens.

The magnifiers

Viewing magnifiers slide into two rails along the sides of the focusing screen frame.

The 5× vertical magnifier has a focusing eyepiece. Adjust it to see sharply the circle marked in the centre of the screen. The adjustment also provides some eyesight compensation, especially for long-sighted users to view without glasses. It is not however sufficient to correct for appreciable short-sightedness; in that case focus either with glasses (when you may not see the whole screen at once) or fit a correction lens in the eyepiece. The required lens diameter is 23.5 mm. This is not available from Leitz; order an appropriate correction lens to your prescription from an optician and get him to cut it down to the right size. Then unscrew the inner retaining ring of the eyepiece (this needs a special 22 mm screw driver), insert the correction lens with its concave side down and carefully screw in the retaining ring again.

The 23 × 35 mm screen image matches a standard slide frame opening, covering slightly less than the film in the film gate, but without parallax or image field loss. The 7 mm circle in the centre (1 mm on earlier models) is about half the diameter of the TTL metering area of the LEICA M6. (In fact it covers the TTL field of the LEICA M5.) It is also an aid to establishing exact reproduction scales in close-ups: place a temporary mm ruler or scale in the centre of the subject and read off the diameter of the circle on that scale. Divide that by 7 to get the reduction.For instance if the circle covers 28 mm on the scale in the picture, 28 ÷ 7 = 4, i.e. a 1:4 reduction.

The 4× eye-level magnifier is in effect a 90° prism finder; push it into the rails from behind only. The image appears slightly smaller than with the vertical magnifier. The eyepiece is not adjustable but takes-correction lenses from +0.5 to −3 diopters [14 118, 14 371 to 14 378 and 14 064].

Camera handling

The rear of the VISOFLEX 3 has a bayonet lens mount like a LEICA M lens. A bayonet locking lever rotates the mount, so there is no need to turn the whole VISOFLEX when attaching it to the camera.

Before mounting the VISOFLEX 3 pull down this lever so that its red dot faces the red dot on the VISOFLEX housing. Push the VISOFLEX against the camera's lens mounting flange, check that it is in full contact all round and push the bayonet locking lever upwards. This secures the VISOFLEX to the camera. To remove, swing the locking lever down and lift off the housing.

The front mount — identical with the lens mounting flange on the camera — now takes various lenses with or without adapter rings (see **The TELYT-V systems** and **The VISOFLEX for close-ups).**

The release lever, protruding up and back from the right of the housing (as seen from behind) operates the mirror. There are three options, selected by a milled knob in the right side. Set its white dot to one of three coloured dots on the housing:

- Black dot: the mirror rises when you press down the lever and returns when you let go.
- Yellow dot: a spring shoots the mirror up at the last moment before the exposure; the mirror returns normally on letting go of the lever. This is useful in telephotography to keep the subject visible in the finder as long as possible (like in a regular SLR camera).
- Turning the knob to the red dot swings and locks the mirror up — for vibration-free releasing in macrophotography etc, but also for TTL metering with the LEICA M6. This setting also keeps the mirror protected when storing the VISOFLEX 3 off the camera.

When you press down the lever an adjustable setting screw in its end pushes against the camera release button. It should release the shutter just after the mirror has fully swung up.

Adjust this with the mirror locked up; in this position the release lever is swung down over the shutter button. Turn the milled collar at the end of the lever to raise or lower the setting screw — its end should be about 1 mm above the release button. Check the setting by turning the mirror control to the yellow dot (spring-driven rise) and trying the release action with the camera empty. You should hear two distinct clicks — first from the spring-powered mirror release and then from the shutter.

A threaded socket next to the release lever takes a cable release. The latter always raises the mirror manually, irrespective of whether the mirror control is set to the yellow or the black dot.

TTL metering with the VISOFLEX

Exposure measurement in the LEICA M6 requires a clear light path between the lens and the white metering spot on the first shutter blind — normally obstructed by the mirror in the VISOFLEX. However, both tele shots and close-ups with the VISOFLEX usually involve reasonably leisurely set-ups with a fixed camera position. With that, there is a way of TTL measurement, even if not as convenient as with a fully functional SLR such as the LEICA R4. Here is how:

(1) Point the camera set-up (with VISOFLEX and lens) at the subject and focus sharply on the screen. Adjust if necessary to centre the subject over the circle in the screen.
(2) Lock up the VISOFLEX mirror out of the way.
(3) Look through the camera's (not the VISOFLEX eyepiece and adjust the shutter speed dial and/or the aperture ring on the lens to balance both LEDs in the finder.
(4) Return the mirror, recheck focusing and image framing, then expose.

Focus on the screen at the full lens aperture. If you set a working aperture for exposure metering, note this, open the lens for the final focusing check (step 4 above) and stop down to the noted value before the exposure.

The upper seascape emphasises depth by careful separation of the foreground, middle distance and background, enhanced by the receding tones from dark to light. In the lower view a distant viewpoint and use of a long-focus lens largely neutralise any effect of depth. *Photos: Heldur J. Netocny.*

The TELYT-V systems

The longer-focus TELYT-V lenses (focal lengths from 200 mm up) are used exclusively with the VISOFLEX 3 housing. These are special outfits for true telephotography, wildlife pictures etc.

The 200 mm TELYT-V f/4 has a screw mount at the rear and fits the VISOFLEX 3 via an adapter ring [16 466]. The latter has appropriate bayonet and screw fittings plus a tripod bush. With this combination the lens focuses down to 3 m or 10 ft, closer still with screw-in extension rings [14 020]. With one such ring the focusing range becomes 3 m to 1.7 m (down to 5½ ft), with two rings from 1.7 to 1.3 m (4½ ft) and with three rings down to 1.13 m or 3¾ ft. This also yields a 1:3.3 reproduction scale, useful for near-range telephotography (see below). On the other hand such piecemeal focusing ranges are not that convenient to handle.

To simplify focusing at the full lens opening and stopping down to any working aperture, the 200 mm TELYT-V has an aperture preselection system with two aperture rings in front of, and behind, the fixed f-stop scale. The front milled ring (with a red dot index) engages at every f-stop and half stop like a normal aperture ring but sets no apertures, only a mechanical stop. The rear ring rotates freely, has a setting index and adjusts the iris diaphragm for the aperture.

For preselection mode turn the rear ring fully to the left (largest aperture) for focusing. Preselect the required working aperture on the front ring — e.g. set the red dot to 8 on the scale for f/8. Immediately before the exposure turn the rear ring to the right to the mechanical stop, closing down the iris to the preset working aperture. Don't turn the ring too hard, or it may carry the preselector ring past the selected stop.

The 280 mm TELYT-V f/4.8 fits directly on the VISOFLEX 3 and focuses from infinity to 3.5 m or 11½ ft, or nearer with extension rings [14 609] with front and rear bayonet fittings. One such ring brings the near focusing limit down to 2.76 m, two rings to 2.33 m and three to 2.06 m (approx. 9, 7¾ and 6¾ respectively). The largest scale is then about 1:5. Like the 200 mm lens the 280 mm TELYT-V has an extending lens hood and apeture preselection. Earlier screw fitting 280mm Telyt needs ring 16 466.

With approximately double the focal length of the 135 mm lenses the 280 mm TELYT-V is the logical first step to telephotography with the VISOFLEX. With only a 50% increase over 135 mm, the 200 mm TELYT-V seems less worth while.

A long focal length and largest aperture reduce depth of field to separate the subject from a busy background. *Photo: Heldur J. Netocny.*

The 400 mm TELYT-V f/6.8 is a long tele system, though comparatively slow. This is acceptable for outdoor wildlife shots on fast film. This TELYT-V is also ideally matched to the fast shooting character of the LEICA: it is comparatively light and can be used for hand-held shooting with the convenient rapid follow-focus mount and shoulder support.

For easier transport the 400 mm TELYT-V splits up into three parts: the lens unit itself with iris diaphragm and follow-focus mount, a mounting tube, and the shoulder support with universal handgrip.

The 560 mm TELYT-V f/6.8 uses the same mounting tube and handgrip with shoulder support as the 400 mm TELYT-V. So if you already have a complete 400 mm lens outfit you need only to get the 560 mm lens unit itself for the second focal length. With a mere 60% focal length difference there seems however little point in having both lenses. The choice is a matter of assessing relative sizes and bulk: that extra 60% in focal length costs only 25% more in weight and 40% more in overall length. On the other hand the 400 mm lens is noticeably handier.

Assemble either lens as follows:

(1) Push the front end of the mounting tube (with bayonet mount and tripod mounting block) into the rear of the lens unit, aligning the two so that the chrome screw head on the tube engages the small notch at the rear of the lens.
(2) Push forward the screw-over ring on the tube and screw firmly over the thread on the lens unit.
(3) Screw the universal hand grip into the rear tripod bush of the tripod mounting block. Check that the locating pin at the top of the handgrip engages a matching hole in the tripod mounting block and that the extending arm points to the rear.
(4) Screw the shoulder support to the end of this extending arm.
(5) Attach the LEICA plus VISOFLEX to the bayonet mount at the rear of the mounting tube. (With these lenses use the VISOFLEX with the 4× eye-level magnifier.)
(6) Push the twin cable release into the long 14 mm hole running from the front to the back in the top of the grip and clamp with the screw at the right. Screw one of the cable release nipples into the VISOFLEX's cable release socket. A twin release is not really essential but the barrel of such units usually fits snugly in the hole of the handgrip; single cable releases are too thin. The plunger can be at the front or back; try both ways to find the more convenient one.
(7) Line up the whole assembly for comfortable loading. Adjust the angle of the extending arm on the grip (slacken off the large milled screw at the bottom) and — after slackening off the large

Ideally, flash shots should hide the fact that they were taken with flash. you often achieve that with a flash off the camera connected by a suitable long synch lead.
Photo: Fritz Meisnitzer.

clamping nut — extend the arm as required. Adjust everything so that the right hand holding the grip pushes the shoulder support into the right shoulder and you can at the same time look comfortably through the VISOFLEX eyepiece.

(8) For upright shots depress the chrome latch at the rear of the mounting tube and rotate the LEICA/VISOFLEX assembly through 90°; it engages in both end positions.

(9) For shooting hold the grip with the right hand as described, with the thumb or index finger on the cable release plunger. Grip the front lens tube with the left hand, the thumb on the focus release button at the left of the tube. On pressing this button you can move the whole tube forward and back for quick focusing. Focus at full aperture, stop down to the required working aperture (after a separate meter reading) and expose by depressing the cable release plunger.

For the steady camera hold support the left elbow on something solid. Alternatively screw the shoulder support to the front of the hand grip; the latter can then stand on a solid surface like the table tripod. (But steady it still with the hand.)

A 60 mm extension tube [14 182] fits between the lens unit and mounting tube to extend the near focusing range. On the 400 mm lens it brings the near limit down from 3.6 m to 2.3 m (7½ ft) with a maximum 1:3.3 scale, on the 560 mm lens from 6.4 to 4 m (13 ft) for a 1:4.7 scale.

A filter slot in the mounting tube takes 2 in. diameter Series 7 filters. Pull back the spring-loaded ring just behind the screw-over ring to expose the slot and insert the filter.

An older version of the hand grip and shoulder support [14 188] is somewhat less convenient than the current model [14 239].

The 800 mm TELYT-V f/6.3 is a specialised system for extreme tele shots. Its weight of some 7 kg or 15½ lb and price put it outside the range of most amateur (and professional) photographers.

Flash is often indispensable in close-up macrophotography. The flash from the side and black background make the orchid stand out dramatically.

Photo: Fritz Meisnitzer.

3075

Near-range telephotography

An interesting aspect of the long-focus TELYT-V lenses is the comparatively long subject distance, even with reasonably large scales of reproduction. At its 3.6 m near limit the 400 mm TELYT-V reaches 1:6.7 or, with the extension tube mentioned above, 1:3.3 at 2.26 m. Even allowing for the distance from the front of the lens to the film plane (50 or 65 cm respectively), this leaves a clear lens/subject distance of 3.1 m or well over 10 ft at a 1:6.7 scale, or 1.7 m (well over 5½ ft) at 1:3.3. With the 560 mm TELYT-V the largest scale is 1:9.3 at a clear 5.8 m (19 ft) distance or 1:4.7 at 3.3 m (nearly 11 ft) away.

This comes in useful in close-ups of small creatures. Thus you optically approach larger insects, bugs etc without getting close enough to scare them away. Butterflies, lizards or frogs tend to stay put for a camera with tele lens (and a photographer well behind) that comes no nearer than 6—7 ft.

However, such shots involve considerable risk of camera shake — so make sure of good light for fast shutter speeds or use fast film and/or flash. Secondly, depth of field at this range depends exclusively on image scale. The depth of field on a caterpillar taken at 1:5 from 13 ft away with the 560 mm lens is about ⅜ in. — the same as when photographed at the same scale with the standard lens and close-up devices (see below) from 8 in away.

The VISOFLEX for close-ups

The 41 mm depth of the VISOFLEX 3 housing also acts as an extension with lenses other than the TELYT-V systems. That covers close-ups at various scales according to the focal lengths involved.
The VISOFLEX again permits precise focusing on the ground glass screen and shows the correct field of view, i.e. acts as a finder. We can consider the following combinations for such close-up and macro applications:

- A helical focusing mount with the 65 mm ELMAR-V f/3.5 or with the separate optical units from other lenses;
- Lenses mounted directly on the VISOFLEX 3;
- A bellow unit with various lenses.

Like the VISOFLEX 3, the helical focusing mounts and bellows are no longer made, but often still obtainable. For the sake of completeness, here are the main elements and possible combinations.

Photo: Heldur J. Netocny.

Combinations with the helical focusing mount

The universal helical focusing mount [16 464] with the 65 mm ELMAR-V fitted is matched to the optical register of the VISOFLEX 3. It therefore permits continuous focusing from infinity down to 0.35 m, just under 14 in. The focusing extension of the helical mount is 28 mm; the scale of reproduction at the nearest setting is 1:2.3, or a 0.43× magnification.

A simple rule to find the magnification from the focusing extension of helical mounts or bellows: divide the extension (forward from the infinity position) by the focal length of the lens; the result is the decimal magnification, or the reciprocal of the reduction (1:...value). For instance with the 28 mm focusing extension: 28 ÷ 65 = 0.43 (or 1:2.3).

The use of the combination is straightforward. Attach the [16 464] mount to the VISOFLEX like a normal bayonet-mounted lens. Then screw the rear thread of the 65 mm ELMAR into the recessed 32.5 mm screw thread of the helical mount. Protect the protruding rear section of the lens (when not on the [16 464] mount) with the push-on cap supplied.

The 65 mm ELMAR-V has an aperture preselection system. Preset the aperture on the front ring according to a meter reading, focus at full aperture (open the rear ring), and stop down to the working aperture just before the exposure.

For still larger reproduction scales, first screw a 27 mm extension tube [16 471] into the helical mount and screw the lens into this tube. The total extension increase is then 55 mm and hence the maximum magnification 1:1.2 or 0.85×. With two such extension tubes the total extra extension (including that of the helical mount) is nearly 82 mm, for a 1.26× magnification. In theory you could go on adding tubes; in practice the bellows unit (see below) is then handier.

The [16 464] mount also takes the lens units of the 90 mm ELMARIT-M f/2.8 and of the 135 mm TELE-ELMAR -M f/4. The 90 mm TELE-ELMARIT-M (without unscrewable lens unit) replaced the ELMARIT-M of this focal length years ago; the latter is however an ideal lens for close-ups with the LEICA M and VISOFLEX. To remove the lens unit from the focusing barrel unscrew by the aperture ring (set the latter to the largest aperture first). Before screwing the lens unit of the 135 mm TELE-EMLAR into the helical mount remove baffles from the rear of the lens (it screens off stray light); refit it before screwing the 135 mm TELE-ELMAR back into its focusing barrel.

With each of these lens units in the helical focusing mount the focusing range extends from infinity downwards. The near limits are 0.5 m (28 in.) with the 90 mm lens and 1 m (40 in.) with the 135 mm, with largest reproduction scales of 1:3.2 and 1:4.8 respectively. The [16 471] extension tubes again allow still closer focusing; the tables (**Close-ups with the VISOFLEX** and **Close-ups with the VISOFLEX and bellows)** sum up available combinations and scales of reproduction.

The lens unit unscrews also from the 135 mm ELMARIT-M f/2.8 and from an ealier version of the 90 mm SUMMICRON-M f/2 |11 123 instead of 11 136, serial Nos. up to 2 997 000]. These lens units fit a different helical focusing mount [16 462] to focus down to 72 cm or 28 in. (90 mm lens, scale 1:6) or to 1.5 m or 5 ft (135 mm lens, scale 1:9). Again, extension tubes [16 474] yield still larger scales. However, the 135 mm lens is less convenient — especially if you have a shorter focal length — as it may need too long a subject distance for a higher magnification.

Lens directly on the VISOFLEX

The front bayonet mount of the VISOFLEX 3 naturally takes any normal LEICA M lens, too. With its 41 mm depth the VISOFLEX then acts as an extension tube. With the shorter lenses (35 and 50mm) the magnification may reach 1.0× but the subject distance is also very short.

Also feasible is a 90 mm lens, e.g. the TELE-ELMARIT-M (scale to 1:2 or 0.5×). In theory the magnification with the 28 mm or 21 mm lens is higher still (nearly 2× with 21 mm); in practice these lenses are not really corrected optically for such an extreme near distance. A normal focal length with the bellows unit yields better definition. Also, the lens/-subject distance with a 21 mm lens becomes too short (an inch or so) for convenient lighting set-ups.

Do not fit older ultrawide-angle lenses with protruding rear mount into the VISOFLEX; they are liable to interfere with the mirror movement.

The bellows unit

For larger-scale close-ups the variable extension of the Bellows-2 unit is more convenient than fixed tube extensions. The bellows unit consists of a rear standard fixed to a rail. Bellows connect the rear with a movable front standard which provides extensions (marked on a scale on the rail) from 0 to 95 mm. The rear standard attaches to the front mount of the VISOFLEX like a lens; the front of the bellows in turn takes various lenses or lens units plus appropriate adapters.

Normally the outfit of the Bellows-2 included an adapter [16 558] to take the 65 mm ELMAR-V or the lens unit of the 90 mm ELMARIT-M and of the 135 mm TELE-ELMAR. With that adapter the minimum bellows extension (0 on the mm scale) is the same as the minimum depth of the helical [16 464] mount and therefore permits focusing from infinity downwards — but nearer than the helical mount. The bellows extension determines the near limit — with reproduction scales to 1.4× (65 mm lens) to 0.7× (135 mm). A special scale on the bellows marks magnifications with the lens unit of the 90 mm ELMARIT-M (from 0 to 1.0).

VISOFLEX 3 with Bellows-2.

Other lenses are usable with alternative adapter rings:

The [16 598] adapter ring for the lens unit of the 90 mm SUMMICRON-M [11 123, serial No. below 2 997 000], of the 135 mm ELMARIT-M, of the 200 mm TELYT-V f/4 and the 280 mm TELYT-V f/4.8. The 90 mm and 135 mm lenses in this case do not focus quite to infinity. With the TELYT-V lenses the focusing range goes from infinity down to a 1:3 or 1:6 scale respectively — which makes this combination with the bellows ideal for the kind of near-range telephotography mentioned earlier.

The [16 596] adapter ring has a LEICA M bayonet mount at the front and thus directly takes M lenses. The scales of reproduction are appreciably larger than when the lenses are mounted on the VISOFLEX.

The [16 590] adapter ring has a 39 mm front screw thread to take lenses of the older screw-mount LEICA models. It is intended for special macro lenses such as the 24 mm Repro-Photar and the 12.5 mm and 50 mm Photar units. These are specifically corrected for optimum performance at high magnifications and hence ideal for extended macrophotography (up to 15× and more).

The same adapter ring takes also enlarging lenses of many makes —

which are again ideally corrected for such magnified reproduction. (The 39 mm screw fitting become a standard when Leitz started using LEICA camera lenses in its enlargers some 50 years ago.) A further [17 672] adapter, fitted in the [16 590] ring, takes the lens unit that unscrews on older versions of the 50 mm SUMMICRON-M [11 817, serial Nos. up to 2 916 800]. The tables again cover the most useful ranges.

To use the bellows unit, mount it on a tripod or other stand (screw into the tripod bush in the base), then attach the VISOFLEX with the camera at the rear. This assembly can rotate on the rear standard for upright or horizontal shots.

The best way of focusing is to extend the bellows first to the intended magnification, move the tripod or stand to the approximate subject distance required and fine focus by moving the whole bellows rail forward and back on the lower mounting block. In effect this matches the distance to the camera setting rather than the other way round. In macrophotography this yields a clearer sharpness change on the screen (with higher focusing precision) than adjusting the bellows extension.

Copying set-ups

From the outset it was part of the LEICA system approach that for certain applications the LEICA camera body should serve simply as a film holder and exposure device (with film transport and shutter) to be incorporated into specialised recording set-ups. This applied particularly to scientific photography, photomicrography, early microfilming practice etc. At various times Leitz developed highly sophisticated equipment for such fields.

The REPROVIT IIa is a typical set-up for such purposes: a base plate with a column and vertically movable camera arm provides for support for copying and close-ups of flat and solid objects. It includes focusing and lighting control as well as other advanced features.

For these applications the LEICA does not even need a viewfinder as reflex or other viewing devices take over that function. The LEICA MD-2 (an M4-P without viewfinder) however has a data recording system to imprint alphanumeric characters, etc, in a 3.5 mm strip along one side of the film image. The system uses a special camera base with a light-tight slot. This slot takes hand-lettered transparent register strips which are thus located in the film gate during the exposure.

Close-ups with the VISOFLEX

Lens	Helical mount (H) + extension tube (e)	Mount extension	Scale of reproduction dec.	1:	Subject dist.* (cm)	Subject field (cm)
65mm ELMAR-V f/3.5	16 464 (H)	min. max.	0 0.4	inf. 2.5	inf 18	— 6 × 9
	16 464 (H) + 16 471 (e)	min. max.	0.4 0.8	2.5 1.2	18 10.5	6 × 9 2.9 × 4.3
	16 464 (H) + 2× 16 471 (e)	min. max.	0.8 1.2	1.2 —	10.5 8	2.9 × 4.3 1.9 × 2.8
90mm ELMARIT-M f/2.8 (lens unit only)	15 464 (H)	min max.	0 0.3	inf. 3.5	inf. 33	— 7.7 × 11.5
	16 464 (H) + 16 471 (e)	min. max.	0.3 0.6	3.5 1.7	33 22	7.7 × 11.5 3.8 × 5.7
	16 464 (H) + 2× 16 471 (e)	min. max.	0.6 0.9	1.7 1.1	22 17	3.8 × 5.7 2.5 × 3.8
135mm TELE-ELMAR f/4 (lens unit only)	16 464 (H)	min. max.	0 0.2	inf. 5	inf. 76.	— 11 × 16.5
	16 464 (H) + 16 471 (e)	min. max.	0.2 0.4	5 2.5	75 43	11 × 16.5 5.6 × 8.4
	16 464 (H) + 2× 16 471 (e)	min. max.	0.4 0.6	2.5 1.7	43 33	5.6 × 8.4 3.8 × 5.7
90mm SUMMICRON-M f/2 (lens unit, up to No.2 997 000)	16 462 (H)	max.	0.11	9	90	20 × 30
	16 462 (H) + 16 474 (e)	min. max.	0.16 0.27	6 3.8	64 61	15 × 22 8.9 × 13.3
	16 462 (H) + 2× 16 474 (e)	min. max.	0.32 0.42	3 2.3	35 28	7.5 × 11.2 5.6 × 8.3
135m ELMARIT-M f/2.8 (lens unit only)	16 462 (H)	max.	0.11	9	135	20 × 30
	16 462 (H) + 16 474 (e)	min. max.	0.11 0.22	9 4.5	135 74	20 × 30 10 × 15
	16 462 (H) + 2× 16 474 (e)	min. max.	0.22 0.33	4.5 3	74 54	10 × 15 7.2 × 10.8
50mm SUMMICRON-M f/2	(directly on VISOFLEX)	Near	0.9	1.1	9	2.7 × 4
35mm SUMMICRON-M f/2	directly on VISOFLEX)	Near	1.2	—	6	2 × 3

*Clear space between front of lens and subject.
Subject distances and subject field sizes are approximate.

Close-ups with the VISOFLEX and Bellows-2

Lens	Extension tube(s)	Scale extension (mm)	Scale of reproduction dec.	1:	Subject dist.*	Subject field
65mm ELMAR-V f/3.5	16 558	0	0	inf.	inf.	—
		95	1.4		10	17 × 25
	16 558 + 16 471	0	0.4	2.5	18	60 × 90
		95	1.85		9	13 × 19
90mm ELMARIT-M f/2.8 (lens unit only)	16 558	0	0	inf.	inf.	—
		95	1.05		17	4 34
	16 558 + 16 471	0	0.3	3.3	33	4 120
		95	1.35		15	4 26
50mm SUMMICRON-M f/2	16 596					
OR		o	1.4		8	17 × 25
50mm SUMMINCRON f/2 (lens unit, Serial No. below 2 915 860)	16 590 + 17 672	95	3.2		6	7.5 × 11.2
50mm PHOTAR	16 590	0	1.3		8	4 27
		95	3.1		6	7.7 × 11.5
	16 590 + 16 615	0	1.8		7.5	13 × 19
		95	3.6		6	6.5 × 9.5
25mm REPRO-PHOTAR	16 590	0	4.0		3	6 × 9
		95	8.0		2.5	3 × 4.5
	16 590 + 16 615	0	5.0		3	4.8 × 7.2
		95	9.0		2.5	2.6 × 4
12.5mm REPRO-PHOTAR	16 590	0	9		1	2.6 × 4
		95	17		1	1.4 × 2.1
	16 590 + 16 615	0	11		1	2.1 × 3.2
		95	19		1	1.2 × 1.8

*Clear space between front of lens and subject.
Subject distances and subject field sizes are approximate.

The Earlier M System

When the LEICA M3 in 1953 began to replace the earlier screw-mount LEICA range, the basic design was a remarkably finalised one. While Leitz did of course update subsequent M models, this made little difference to handling and use. The operation described so far for the LEICA M6 and M4-P therefore applies very largely also to previous versions. This chapter sums up those features and details in which the earlier LEICA M models differ from the present ones.

Rangefinder variations

Previous to the LEICA M4-P the viewfinder did not include bright-line frames for the 28 mm and 75 mm lenses. The 50 mm frame and the 90 mm frame therefore appeared on their own when you mounted those lenses on the camera. However, Leitz will fit the extra frames to an earlier camera (other than M1 or M3) if it is returned to a Leitz Service Agent.

One reason why the LEICA M3 cannot be thus adapted is its different finder line-up. This finder showed the image in almost natural visual size (rather than reduced to 0.7×). However that meant that the finder could not cover the view of the 35 mm lenses — neither was there room for the 35 mm bright-line frame. The M3 thus had finder frames only for the 50 mm, 90 mm and 135 mm lenses.

There were two ways of using 35 mm lenses: either with a separate brilliant finder (like the current ones for the 21 mm and 28 mm lenses) — or with special finder-adapted versions of the 35 mm lenses. These had a finder attachment similar to the attachment on the 135 mm ELMARIT-M, except that it made the finder image smaller rather than larger. With such an attachment the finder view of the LEICA M3 was very similar to that of the LEICA M6.

In view of its larger optical scale the M3 rangefinder also had a longer effective base length — virtually the physical base length of 69 mm, which thus meant greater ranging and focusing accuracy. Many LEICA photographers still regard the LEICA M3 as the most user-friendly model of the whole M range — except for using 35 mm lenses. (With the special finder attachment these were somewhat cumbersome.)

The earliest LEICA M3 had no finder frame selector lever.

A special rangefinder feature of the LEICA M3 (except earliest versions) and of the M2 is an optical depth-of-field check. The central rectangular rangefinder field has a small narrow cut-out in its bottom edge and a larger one in the top edge. When the double outlines of a not quite precisely focused object are separated by not more than the width of the lower narrow cut-out, that object is within the depth of field of the standard 50 mm lens at f/5.6. The wider cut-out at the top similarly indicates the permissible focusing error at f/16.

The LEICA M1 only has a viewfinder with fixed bright-line frames for the 35 mm and 50 mm lenses — no rangefinder and no finder frame selector. As a bare camera body for copying and other specialised equipment set-ups, the LEICA MD, MDa and MD-2 have no finder at all.

The fully developed LEICA M3. Note the two dots in the centre of the rewind knob (which is pulled up clear of the rangefinder housing to operate) which indicate by their rotation that the film is winding on properly after loading. The slot in the shutter speed dial engages with a pin in the exposure meter setting wheel to couple the meter to the shutter speeds of the camera. The semi-circular guard round the lens-bayonet release button was a feature of the M3 that was discontinued in later M cameras.

LEICA M3 with earlier form of MR meter mounted. Note that the meter switch is a push knob on the side. With the advent of the M4 the switch was changed to a slide on the top of the meter to avoid fouling of the rewind crank of the M4.

LEICA M2 with 35 mm f/2.8 SUMMARON, 50 mm f/2.8 ELMAR and 90 mm f/2.8 ELMARIT. The LEICA M2 was originally conceived as a simplified M3 suitable for amateurs which is why the slower lenses were featured as forming the basic outfit. Bright-line frames were provided in the viewfinder for 35, 50 and 90 mm lenses as against the 50, 90 and 135 mm of the M3. However this view-finder became the basis of all subsequent M viewfinders with its ability to accommodate winder angle lenses. Note the louvred window for illuninating the viewfinder bright-line frames compared to the plain window of the M3. With the later introduction of the 135 mm f/2.8 ELMARIT with its special viewfinder attachment the M2 was able to accommodate a 135 mm lens. The external frame counter disc under, and coaxial with the wind-on lever can be clearly seen. Later models of the M2 were equipped with a selftimer.

LEICA M1. Based on the M2 but without rangefinder or delayed action and with bright-line frames for 35 and 50 mm only; intended mainly for use with the VISOFLEX.

LEICA M4. This had bright-line frames for 35, 50, 90 and 135 mm lenses. It also had a rewind crank instead of a knob; the crank was angled so that it would not foul the exposure meter when mounted. The elbowed rewind lever with the hinged plastic finger grip was also introduced for the first time with the M4.

LEICA M4 rear view. The two flash contact sockets provided on earlier M cameras, one for electronic flash and one for flash bulbs, can be seen with their plastic sealing caps fitted; also the film speed reminder disc, common to all M cameras prior to the M6.

LEICA M4-2. The main differences compared with the M4 were the provision of a hot-shoe and the omission of a selftimer.

Exposure metering and setting

All LEICA M models other than the M6 (and M5 — see below) have provision for coupling with the LEICAmeter MR exposure meter or earlier LEICAmeter versions. (See LEICAmeter MR on page 68) The coupling element is again a stud on the meter setting wheel that engages a notch in the camera's shutter speed dial. Very early LEICA M3 models had a different shutter speed range (1/15, 1/50, 1/100 etc sec).

A previous LEICAmeter MR had a differently shaped meter switch, the still earlier LEICAmeter MC a selenium cell with plug-in booster cell. Handling was similar to the present version.

For flash the LEICA M4 and earlier M models had no hot shoe contact but two flash sockets in the rear (as in the M4-P). The sockets in the M1, M2 and M3 take special LEICA plugs; a bayonet-type fitting secures them in position. They also take adapters for standard coaxial plugs.

The LEICA M5 with its built-in TTL meter is similar in principle (though neither in design nor in operation) to the TTL system of the M6. The M5 uses a cadmium sulphide cell on a swivelling arm. Tensioning the shutter swings this arm into position just in front of the shutter to read the light coming through the lens almost in the film place. Immediately before the exposure the cell swings out of the way. It also does so (for protection) when you remove the lens. The meter uses an electro-mechanical galvanometer system and a more elaborate needle and scale display arrangement — all of which make the LEICA M5 noticeably bulkier (and heavier) than the M4 or M6.

Operation is only slightly more involved than with the M6. The film speed setting is a dial on the camera top. A long horizontal white slot is visible below the finder, in the slot is a horizontal black bar intersected by an oblique setting pointer (running from the top left to bottom right). You can adjust this setting pointer by the shutter speed and film speed. The shutter setting is visible at the left in the finder. When you point the camera at the subject (after tensioning the shutter), a second meter needle travels from left to right. When this needle and the setting pointer intersect on the black bar, the exposure setting is correct. If they do not intersect on the bar, adjust the aperture (which controls the meter needle movement, responding to the light coming through the lens) or the shutter — which moves the setting or matching pointer. If the meter needle fails to move the light is too weak, the shutter not tensioned or the lens cap still on the lens.

With slow films you may have to move the shutter speed dial past the B setting to match the setting pointer to the meter needle. The dial then indicates the length of a time exposure needed with the aperture in use. A calculator dial in the camera back provides conversion values at other apertures.

Certain lenses are not compatible with TTL metering in the LEICA M5. The problem is similar to that of the M6 but in the M5 the rear of the lens may physically foul the meter cell on its swinging arm. Leitz adapts such lenses so that they do not actuate the meter cell when you fit them on the camera. You then have to measure the exposure first with a normal lens and then switch to the special wide-angle one.

Film loading, transport and unloading

Film loading in the LEICA M1, M2 and M3 differs only slightly from the procedure for the M4 and M6. Instead of the fixed split take-up spool these models have a removable regular spool. Before loading pull out this spool, push the film end (emulsion side out) underneath the leaf spring of the spool core, then insert the film cartridge and take-up spool in their two compartments in the camera. The film needs more careful positioning, apart from that, loading and advancing to the first frame involves the same steps as with the current models.

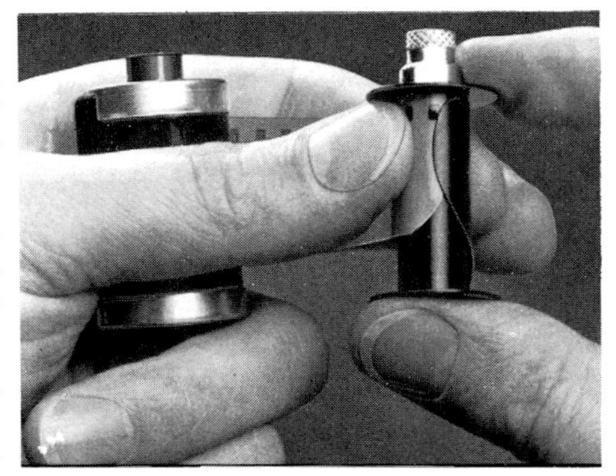

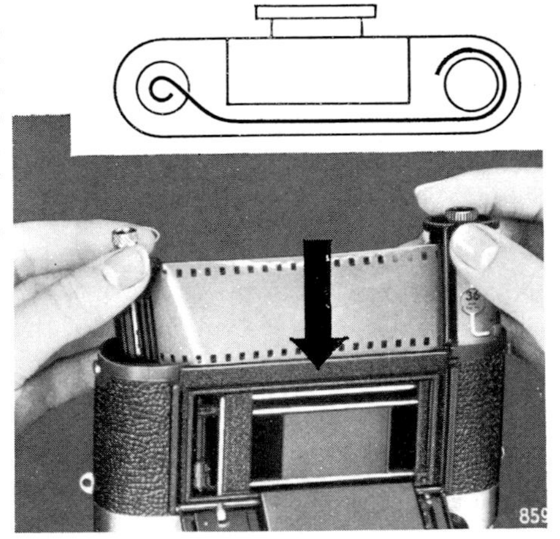

Loading M3, M2 and M1 cameras with their separate take-up spool. Hold the take-up spool in the right hand and the cassette in the left, both with the spool knobs pointing up. Push the film leader under the clamping spring of the take-up spool as far as it will go with the perforated film edge lying flush against the spool flange as shown. Draw out just enough of the film leader from the cassette to enable the cassette and take-up spool to be inserted into the camera. The milled spool knobs should still point upwards, i.e. to the base of the camera. The cassette and take-up spool must be pushed fully home to ensure that the film lies properly between the guides. Check that the position of the film corresponds to that shown on the diagram with the matt emulsion side facing the lens; the take-up spool winds the film with emulsion side out. The teeth of the transport sprocket should engage the film perforations. If necessary slowly work the transport lever until the teeth engage.

A carefully set up still life, shot with a long focus lens at full aperture, to emphasise the flowers by differential focusing. *Photo: Dr M. Beisert.*

see P. 140

M1 and M2 counter has to be manually set after loading film

Soon after the M4, Leitz issued a rapid film loading system also for the older M models. It consisted of a special take-up spool to replace the regular spool and a film locating aid to be installed inside the camera base plate. This outfit [14 260] upgraded the LEICA M1 to M3 models to the loading convenience of the M4 and M5.

The M5 is loaded similarly to the M6 but the removable take-up spool resembles the spool of the [14 260] outfit. Push the film leader from above into one of the slits surrounding the spool core.

The exposure sequence and film transport are similar on all M models. The winding lever on the M1 to M3 had no swivelling plastic end piece. The very first LEICA M3 always needed a double lever swing to advance the film — no option of a single larger swing.

The LEICA M2 (except for the earliest version) to M5 models (including M4 but not M4-2 and M4-P) have a selftimer on the camera front, just below the rewind clutch lever. It is usable with all shutter speeds except B.

To set the selftimer, tension the shutter and pull down the selftimer lever to a second audible click. (The lever should be at least horizontal or point slightly downwards.) The lever also uncovers a small chrome button. Release the selftimer by pressing that button. Once the escapement starts running (audible by a buzzing noise) you cannot stop it — but you can release manually before the selftimer.

Long tele lenses can make long-range close-ups possible. At its near limit of 3.6 m the 400 mm TELYT-V f/6.8 yields a 1:6.7 scale. *Photo: Dr M. Beisert.*

The delay is adjustable: it is about 5 sec with the lever horizontal and up to 10 sec with the lever pulled down fully. The selftimer is useful not only for the classical group portrait with the photographer in the picture — but also for shake-free releasing of a manually supported camera. Start the selftimer and then concentrate on holding the camera still — without worrying over first or second pressures on the release, indeed without pressing on the release at all.

Except for the M5, unloading is also the same for all models. The M1 to M3 however have a rewind knob instead of a crank. After moving the rewind clutch lever to 'R' (on the early M2 after pressing the button) pull up the rewind know and turn it to rewind the film. The M5 has a crank, but in the camera base. The M5 does not take self-opening Leitz Type N cassettes (see FILM HANDLING chapter).

Older M lenses

One aspect of optical evolution is that from time to time new and improved lens designs replace older or existing ones. Apart from optical improvements in performance, lens speed or filter size, some handling aspects may change, too. Many of these changes need no further description but some older lenses are worth noting:

The 15 mm Hologon f/8 is a Carl Zeiss ultrawide-angle lens in a special version for the LEICA M. It covers a horizontal 100° angle without optical distortion and is not coupled with the LEICA rangefinder (not really necessary in view of the Hologon's immense depth of field.) It is not usable with TTL metering. The Hologon focuses down to 0.2 m and was intended for certain applications in architectural photography. It was supplied with a special brilliant finder; a graduated filter (neutral density, decreasing from the centre outwards) was recommended to compensate the light loss from the centre to the edges (inevitable with this angle of view).

The 21 m Super-Angulon f/3.4 and f/4 are slower forerunners of the 21 mm ELMARIT-M. Super-Angulon-M lenses of serial No. below 2 473 251 have an extended rear mount that protrudes into the TTL metering light path of the LEICA M6.

The 35 mm SUMMICRON-M f/2 existed in several earlier versions, including the models with finder attachment for the LEICA M3. The 35 mm SUMMILUX-M f/1.4 was also available with this finder attachment. Some twenty years ago there were slower 35 mm SUMMARON f/2.8 and (up to 1960) f/3.5 lenses — both also with finder attachments.

The 50 mm SUMMICRON had numerous variants, too. The immediate predecessor of the current [11 819] lens is the [11 817] version (serial Nos. up to 2 915 860) without a lever extension on the focusing mount.

However, the lens unit unscrewed for use on the [16 507] close-up mount (see **Near focusing aids** below). Prior to 1970 there was a 50 mm SUMMICRON with dual focusing mount [11 918] that could be switched to a near range (between about 3 and 1½ ft with a maximum 1:7.5 scale). A separate finder attachment adapted the camera's rangefinder to the near range. At the time of the first LEICA M3 (1954) there was also a collapsible 50 mm SUMMICRON which was specially compact on the camera but had to be extended before shooting.

Further standard lenses included — between 1957 and 1974 — a **50 mm ELMAR f/2.8** and, up to 1961, even **f/3.5.** Today such slow standard lenses are associated only with inexpensive 35 mm cameras.

Some past LEICA lenses were collapsible, such as this 50 mm ELMAR f/2.8.

The 90 mm ELMARIT f/2.8 existed up to 1974 alongside the more compact TELE-ELMARIT-M of the same focal length. With its removable lens unit the 90 mm ELMARIT is ideal for close-ups with the VISOFLEX 3 and the [16 464] focusing mount. In this focal length there were also several versions of an ELMAR f/4, nearly all with removable lens unit usable on the VISOFLEX with an older [16 467] helical mount. there was also a collapsible version; when retracted, this protruded no further on the camera than the standard lens.

The 135 mm ELMAR f/4, and 135 mm HEKTON f/4.5 both proceeding the TELE-ELMAR, were noticeable longer, already had a removable lens unit unit but needed a different adapter ring [16 472] to fit on the VISOFLEX. This ring then screws into the helical [16 464] mount or the regular [16 471] extension tube.

There were numerous earlier 200 mm, 400 mm and 560 mm TELYT lenses. The **400 mm TELYT f/5.6** and **560 mm f/5.6** were exlusively intended for use with the TELEVIT follow-focus mount — more convenient than the present follow-focus mount but also considerably heavier and more expensive. These drawbacks rather outweighed the advantage of the mere half an f-stop in lens speed over the current f/6.8 versions.

Near focusing aids

Before the SLR became widespread, Leitz provided various near focusing aids for the rangefinder LEICA. Some of these adapted the rangefinder to nearer focusing ranges, others acted as mechanical distance gauges to establish exact subject distances for specific extension units.

Thus the [16 507] close-up mount, combined with the lens unit of the older [11 818] 50 mm SUMMICRON f/2, covered a range down to a 1:7.5 scale, fulfilling the same functions as the dual-range 50 mm SUMMICRON.

Copying gauges, usable with most 50 mm lenses, covered A4, A5 and A6 formats for copying. An extension collar (between the camera and lens) took extending legs which outlined the exact subject field and kept the camera at the correct distance from the original being copied. This was a compact and portable outfit intended for straightforward copying in libraries and museums. Close-up stands with extension units and distance gauges for 1:1 copying relied on similar set-ups.

The VISOFLEX 2, a forerunner of the VISOFLEX 3, took the same helical mounts and extension tubes as the model 3. Still earlier VISOFLEX 1 reflex housings were longer and needed different adapters. The VISOFLEX 1 system included a bellows unit 1 with 140 mm extension.

Camera and Lens Care

For all its precision engineering, the LEICA is a tool and not, except among collectors, a showpiece. The camera is tough — on expeditions and extended travel LEICA cameras have stood up to extremes of climate. Not surprisingly they collected quite a few knocks. On the other hand a camera treated sensibly will maintain its precision and perfect functioning longer than one constantly exposed to dust, moisture and mechanical stress.

Care of the LEICA covers three aspects: mechanics, optics and, for the M6, electronics.

Mechanical care

If you are constantly using a camera professionally, occasional scratches and knocks are unavoidable. The chrome finish (including black chrome since about 1970) is normally quite abrasion resistant — unlike the black lacquer of earlier versions. (I know professionals who proudly carry a LEICA with the entire black finish worn off down to the brass underneath.) But knocks, scraping against sharp edges etc in time leave their tracks in the toughest chrome plating, too. So when I am not actually using my LEICA I prefer to carry it in a soft leather case.

Guard the camera also against dust, moisture and especially fine sand. On the beach and especially in the desert sand dust penetrates everywhere, even inside the camera. If you have no case, store the camera on such travels in a waterproof and dustproof plastic container. For example, sealed Ewa underwater housings provide excellent protection against dust and of course splashes.

Dust on the camera just looks neglectful. Inside the camera it also shows up in the pictures, not to mention what it can do to the precision mechanism. So "dedust" the camera regularly. Small battery-powered vacuum cleaners do a good job of that — especially in the film chambers and the space between the lens mount and the shutter. But do not poke a pointed nozzle into the shutter curtain. A small blower brush will also do but needs more thorough handling as it blows the dust somewhere else rather than getting rid of it. If you can afford the time, clean out the camera carefully every time you load a film.

Avoid handling a camera with greasy hands. Clean grease and other soiling carefully off the LEICA with a soft rag, but do not use solvents (which can cause trouble if they get inside the camera).

Cameras have been known to get wet. The mechanism suffers most afterwards, when damp or wet components start to corrode, especially after immersion in salt water. One first-aid measure that has been suggested for such a case is to rinse the camera thoroughly in fresh (non-salt) water straightaway and to get it to a repair service station immersed in water. This may limit the damage. The camera obviously must be stripped down completely; if this is done soon enough, even more delicate components may escape corrosion damage. (The electronics is a different story. Be sure to remove batteries from a soaked LEICA M6.)

A basic rule for all mechanical camera components is that items that should move must do so freely or engage positively. There are not many adjustments that a LEICA user can carry out, so in case of malfunction never use force, don't touch the shutter curtains with the fingers, get the camera to a Leitz service agency as soon as possible.

Lens care

For spotless and clear images the lens should be spotless too. Preferably keep it clean by putting on the lens cap whenever you are not shooting, and also fitting a rear cap when removing the lens from the LEICA. In the long run fitting and removing lens caps is less trouble than removing finger prints and other dirt from the lens surfaces.

Remove a finger print by carefully wiping it off the glass with a piece of chamois leather. Preferably dab it off (never rub over the whole lens surface); you can help by breathing on it very gently if necessary. In the absence of a chamois lether use a clean and well washed handkerchief. On the other hand avoid cleaning fluids and impregnated cleaning tissues unless they are expressly designed for photographic lens cleaning. These look very like cleaning tissues for spectacles, which are less suitable for photo lenses.

Remove dust and other foreign matter by blowing it off — wiping can scratch the glass. A small blower brush (as used also for cleaning the camera's film chambers) is useful — but keep it or carry it in the camera bag inside a dustproof plastic bag. An imperfectly clean blower brush can apply more dirt to the lens surface than it removes. That applies equally to chamois leathers used to remove fingerprints. Store such leather patches in a dust-free plastic container, for instance a film can. Don't blow dust away by mouth, you can easily blow tiny splashes onto the lens surface.

Apart from lens units that unscrew, lens components are not intended to be dismantled. Don't screw lens units in too tightly either, that could cause damage to the aperture ring or its internal linkages by the excessive force needed to unscrew.

Camera electronics

Electric components of the LEICA M6 and of the winder etc are even less accessible for the user than mechanical ones. Electronic camera malfunction usually requires replacement of the printed circuit — a matter for professional servicing. But batteries need proper care, too.

When the silver oxide or lithium button cells in the M6 are exhausted, the metering function and signals fail. But during use, and especially during prolonged storage, small amounts of chemical matter may leak out of the cell and corrode or at least impair the contacts in the battery compartment. If a cell appears to fail prematurely, first clean the battery compartment contacts and the cell itself — it may then continue working for weeks or even months.

Check the contacts also when changing batteries. The spring pressing on the button cell must be shiny. Chemicals leaking out of mercury cells (in the LEICA M5 or the LEICAmeter) or out of alkaline button cells used in the M6 can corrode the contact spring. To clean it, take a tiny piece of finest grade emery cloth in a pair of tweezers and polish the spring shiny again. (I prefer to avoid alkaline button cells.)

When using a pair of silver oxide cells in the M6 always replace them together — never combine a fresh and partly used cell.

In the winder and flash units use either alkaline or rechargeable nicad cells. Avoid ordinary zinc-carbon torch batteries; they usually leak when they near exhaustion and play havoc with contacts.

Check the battery sets in the winder and flash unit regularly. At the slightest sign of leakage change the whole battery set. Alkaline cells are supposed to be leakproof; they are not if operating conditions initiate chemical reactions that generate internal cell pressure. That can happen if one cell of a set is exhausted and the other cells push a reverse voltage through it. (Another reason why battery sets should be replaced as a whole, never piecemeal, and why mixing fresh and nearly exhausted cells can cause trouble.)

If the camera, winder or flash units are not in use for long periods, remove all batteries and store them separately. That also avoids possibly harmful leakage inside equipment.

LEICA History

The more than sixty years of LEICA evolution form an important chapter of camera engineering history. This is also a subject of intense interest to individual historians, camera collectors and world-wide LEICA historical clubs and societies, who meticulously follow every detail of the thousands of equipment items and accessories produced during this period. It is very much an esoteric theme. The listing below is a kind of family tree to sum up on the one hand the design versatility and on the other the logic of its development.

From prototype to the LEICA 1

1912/1913: The proto-LEICA, hand-built by Oskar Barnack, already had the main body shape of the later LEICA, a permanently built-in retractable lens with swivelling lens cap (the shutter was not yet self-capping), two shutter speeds (approx. $^1/_{25}$ and $^1/_{50}$ sec) and coupled shutter tensioning and film transport. Barnack made two of these cameras, and may some years later have produced a further improved version. There are also a number of modern replicas.

1923: Preproduction pilot run — 31 cameras with permanently fitted, retractable 50 mm Leitz Anastigmat f/3.5 lens and shutter speeds from $^1/_{20}$ to $^1/_{500}$ sec. Built-in frame or optical finder (individual cameras of this pilot run differed slightly in detail), with accessory shoe.

1925: LEICA I (also known as model A in the US) — with built-in fixed 50 mm Leitz Anastigmat f/3.5 lens (later named Elmax) and, from 1926 onwards, f/3.5 ELMAR; also with 50 mm Hektor f/2.5 around 1930. Shutter speeds from $^1/_{25}$ (later $^1/_{20}$) to $^1/_{500}$ sec, optical finder. Production of the first seven years from 1925 to 1931 totalled some 55 000 units.

1926: Compur-LEICA (model B) — with fixed ELMAR lens in a Compur leaf shutter (to $^{1}/_{300}$ sec). First version had small setting dial, later (1928) rim-set. Total production 1600 units.

1930. LEICA I (model C) — first LEICA with interchangeable screw-mounted lenses. The latter were individually matched to each camera.

1931: LEICA I — with standardised lens mount (28.8 mm optical register), making lenses interchangeable between different camera bodies, too. Leitz later fitted some of the earlier LEICA C models with a standard mount. Altogether about 10 000 models C were made between 1930 and 1933.

Years of growth: the pre-war LEICA system

The standard lens mount stimulated rapid expansion of the available lens selection and especially of a wide-ranging accessories system.

1932: LEICA Standard (model E) — resembled the model C but had an extending rewind knob. Initially in black, from 1933 onwards also with chrome finish. Production continued until 1940 (with a few cameras even up to 1950), totalling just over 27 000 units.

1932: LEICA II (model D) — first LEICA with built-in coupled rangefinder. Originally finished in black, later (1933) also in chrome. About 51 000 units were made up to 1940, a few hundred more up to 1948.

1933: LEICA III (model F) — A LEICA II with additional slow shutter speeds from 1 to $^{1}/_{20}$ sec and carrying strap eyelets. Production over 76 000 up to 1939.

1934: LEICA 250 model FF) — basically a LEICA III with enlarged film chambers to take special cartridges holding 10 m of film for 250 exposures. The very first models had no slow speeds (like the LEICA II); from 1934 onwards the fastest shutter speed was $^{1}/_{1000}$ sec (model GG). A few models were also fitted with electric motor drives. Production up to 1942

totalled under 1000 units (plus a few odd ones later).

1935: LEICA IIIa (model G) — fastest shutter speed $^{1}/_{1000}$ sec, otherwise like the LEICA III but with adjustable rangefinder eyepiece. 1938: LEICA IIIb — improved IIIa with twin eyepiece for the viewfinder and rangefinder.

The post-war period: screw-mount LEICA with die-cast bodies

In 1939 Leitz started producing LEICA models with a slightly longer die-cast body and various mechanical improvements. This range ran until nearly ten years after the appearance of the M models.

1939: LEICA IIIc — similar to the model IIIb in specification, underwent numerous minor (mainly internal) changes between 1939 and 1951, during which period Leitz produced over 130 000 units (almost half of them in 1949 and 1950). A speeded up shutter mechanism provided a shortest exposure of $^{1}/_{30}$ sec in the slow speed range.

1939: LEICA IIId — special version of the IIIc with built-in selftimer, similar to that of the later IIIf. Only about 500 cameras were made of this version.

1948: LEICA IIc — simpler version of the IIIc with a top shutter speed of $^{1}/_{500}$ sec and without slow speeds but with a mounting plate for a slow-speed dial on the front of the body (see **Special sizes and conversions).** Production ran to about 11 000 units.

1949. LEICA Ic — stripped-down IIc with two finder shoes instead of the viewfinder and rangefinder assembly. Intended as a successor to the LEICA Standard for scientific photography and related applications that require a LEICA body but no finder system, for instance for installation in macrophoto, copying, photomicrographic and instrument recording set-ups.

1950: LEICA IIIf — based on IIIc but with fully adjustable flash synchronisation and selector dial for flash firing delays to match different flash types. Film speed indicator in winding knob. Original version)1950—51) had shutter speeds of $^{1}/_{30}$, $^{1}/_{40}$, $^{1}/_{60}$ etc sec and black synchronising scale, later version from 1952 had a revised shutter speed range of $^{1}/_{25}$, $^{1}/_{50}$, $^{1}/_{75}$ etc sec and a red synchronising scale. A selftimer was built into models from 1954 onwards. Screw-mount LEICA with largest production volume — around 185 000 units, including the first cameras to be assembled in Canada.

1951: LEICA IIf — simpler version of the IIIf with no slow speeds and (unitl 1954) with $^{1}/_{500}$ sec as top speed. As with the IIIf there were versions with black and with red synchronising dials, but none with selftimer. Total production about 35 000 cameras.

1952: LEICA If — similar to Ic but flash synchronised. Only about 1000 of the nearly 17 000 cameras of this model still had the older style black synchronising dial.

1956/57: LEICA IIIg — the most advanced of all the screw-mount LEICAS and also the swan song of the screw-mount range. Appearing after the M3, it incorporated certain of the latter's improvements in a LEICA IIIf body, such as the parallax-corrected bright-line finder with frames for the 50 and 90 mm lenses, internal flash contact wihtout need for synchronising dial, geometric shutter speed scale (constant double/half intervals) and film type indicator in the camera back. About 100 IIIg models (of a total production of more than 40 000) were supplied in black finish, for the first time since before the war. Some IIIg models were also assembled at the Canadian Leitz factory. Special versions included abotu a dozen models without slow speeds (LEICA IIg) and allegedly also a few trial cameras with M-type bayonet lens mount.

1957: LEICA Ig — based on the IIIg but without finder optics and without selftimer, again for installation in laboratory and other recording set-ups. Total production about 6000 units.

The modern M models

The LEICA underwent its biggest design change with the M3 in 1954. This not only switched at last from the traditional screw lens mount to a bayonet fitting but also introduced a fully integrated combined view- and rangefinder with multiple image frames for different focal lengths, a winding lever to replace the obsolete winding knob, the hinged back panel and other modifications. Apart from built-in exposure metering it closely resembled the LEICA M6 in shape and features. The LEICA M models ran through numerous development phases with external and internal changes.

1954: LEICA M3 — this differed from all other LEICA M models in its almost 1:1 visual finder magnification with bright-line frames for the 50, 90 and 135 mm lenses. With over 235 000 units the M3 also holds the production volume record for LEICA camera models. Changes between 1954 and 1966 (all still designated M3): switch to geometric shutter speeds in 1957, finder frame selector lever added in 1955, various design changes to the winding lever, carrying strap eyelets etc.

1956: LEICA MP — special model for press photographers, with LEICAVIT MP rapid winding unit and finder frame selector but without selftimer and with manually set frame counter. Only about 450 cameras were produced. An MP2 version (1957) was equipped to take a motor winder (not produced by Leitz).

1958: LEICA M2 — downmarket alternative to the M3 with lower finder magnification (0.7×) but larger finder field and bright-line frames for 35 mm, 50 mm and 90 mm lenses. Initially without selftimer. Simpler manually set frme counter as on the MP. Production up to 1967 just under 86 000 units, 1600 cameras being made in Canada.

1959: LEICA M1 — similar to M2 mechanically but without rangefinder; fixed bright-line frames for 35 mm and 50 mm in finder. Intended for scientific, etc, applications as a camera body in set-ups using the VISOFLEX reflex housing.

1964: LEICA MD — taking the M1 a logical step further, the MD followed the Ig in having no viewfinder at all. But fitted with data imprinting facility, taking register strips inserted through the base plate. Production about 3300 cameras.

1967: LEICA M4 — combined the best features of past LEICA M models with the M2 finder (but finder frames for the 35, 50, 90 and 135 mm lenses). Self-resetting frame counter as on M3, new shape of winding lever, simplified film loading as on current M6, rewind crank instead of former knob. Special M4 MOT or M4M version had coupling elements for an American-made motor winder. Last rangefinder LEICA to be produced in comparatively large numbers — nearly 59 000 units up to 1975, including 2600 in Canada.

1966/67: LEICA MDa — updated MD with mechanical features like M4 but without finder, finder frame selector, or selftimer.

1971: LEICA M5 first LEICA with built-in exposure meter, using a CdS cell moving in front of the shutter on an arm. Hence not only first 35 mm rangefinder camera on the market with TTL exposure measurement but also first to use central spot readings. Shutter speed dial mechanically coupled with meter mechanism; latter however made the M5 the bulkiest and heaviest-ever rangefinder LEICA camera.

1973: LEICA CL — designed in Wetzlar but made in Japan, the LEICA CL was a rangefinder camera but apart from the M-type bayonet mount had little in common with the tradition or the style of the LEICA M models. Lower-price amateur camera with TTL metering similar to the M5. Minolta produced some 35 000 CLs for Leitz plus a further number for the Japanese market as the Leitz-Minolta. This eventually evolved into the Minolta CLE with TTL exposure automation.

1976: LEICA M4-2 — resumed production (almost exclusively in Canada) in response to demand for more M4 cameras. Differs from the

previous M4 in being equipped with coupling elements to take a motor winder, with a hot shoe but without selftimer. The **M4-P** of 1980 is virtually the same camera but with additional finder frames.

1977: LEICA MD-2 — LEICA MDa updated to level of M4-2 with winder coupling facility; black finish.

1984: LEICA M6 — current model with built-in selective (large spot) TTL exposure metering in an M4 body. Launched in black chrome finish, but silver chrome version introduced in 1986.

Collectors' and other special versions

LEICA collectors are of course after rare models and variations. Specially valuable are not only models produced in small numbers (e.g. LEICA 250, Compur-LEICA, IIId) but also low serial numbers of the very first models.

Other LEICAS of rarity value are specially engraved models and versions in coloured finish. Special engravings appeared on cameras produced for armed forces of various countries, modified models (arctic versions with shutters running in ball bearings, special cameras supplied to NASA) etc. A series of some 400 LEICA IIIa cameras assembled in 1949 and 1950 in the then French-occupied Saar area were also appropriately marked.

Collectors' items further include Jubilee models — some with a '50 Jahre' engraving (LEICA M4, M5 and CL in 1975) — and a gold plated LEICA M4-2 to mark the 100th anniversary of the birth of Oskar Barnack (1979). These special issues, avidly bought by speculators, have no more relevance to picture taking than stamp collecting has to writing letters. (The inspiration for this limited-edition fad, enthusiastically copied by other camera makers, may have been a lizard-skin covered, gold-plated Luxury LEICA marketed in 1929.)

Special sizes and conversions

LEICA models for smaller image sizes were produced for special purposes. Best known was the half-frame LEICA 72 for microfilming applications, assembled mainly in Canada in 1954 and 1955. This IIIa body had an 18 × 24 mm film gate, masked down finder and modified film transport and frame counter. A model MD-22 — a half-frame 18 × 24 mm LEICA MD-2 — was announced in 1976 but never went into production.

In the 1930s there was a 24 × 24 mm version of the LEICA Standard for mass X-ray fluorography, the first LEICA with a rewind crank. In the 1960s Leitz supplied a 24 × 27 mm LEICA MD Post to the German post office to record telephone subscribers' meter readings.

During the currency of screw-mounted LEICA models Leitz undertook to convert simpler models to more advanced versions, installing interchangeable lens mounts (in the earliest LEICA I), a rangefinder and, later, flash synchronisation (IIIg-syn and IIIb-syn models). Postwar cameras with die-cast body could be upgrded (with some reservations) to the more advanced models If to IIIf).

The construction of the LEICA M models does not permit conversion of earlier versions to later models. The only retrofitting available is installation of the additional finder frames (for 28 mm and 75 mm) of the M4-P and M6 in the LEICA M2, M4 (including M4 MOT), M4-2 and M5.

Technical Glossary

Readers of this book are assumed to know something of the basics of photography, but not necessarily to be experts. To most photographers the terminology is fairly obvious. These brief definitions of frequently recurring technical items should clarify terms that may occasionally not be obvious.

Acutance: Also known as edge sharpness; degree of sharpness with which a film renders ideal high-contrast edges or outlines (black/white edges). The term acutance applies primarily to films but also affects, like lens definition, the degree to which a film image can be satisfactorily enlarged. Low-speed films, especially thin-emulsion ones, usually yield images of high acutance.

Aperture: Variable opening in the lens, controls light intensity passing through the lens. One of the control parameters of exposure (the other is shutter speed). A control on the lens indicates aperture settings on a scale (1 — 1.4 — 2 2.8 — 4 — 5.6 — 8 — 11 — 16 — 22 — 32) where the amount of light passed doubles with each lower aperture value (f-value, usually expressed as, for example, f/1.4) or is halved with each higher value. Thus high f-values are small lens openings; they are inversely proportional to the diameter of the opening. They are also relative; with any lens a given f-value (in theory) passes the same amount of light. On LEICA lenses the aperture ring also engages at half-stop settings, i.e. intermediate points on the above scale. With a few lenses the largest aperture may be such as intermediate value (e.g. f/3.5).

B setting: Setting on the shutter speed dial for long time exposures (longer than 1 sec). Pressing the release button opens the shutter (only the first shutter blind runs down) which then stays open until you let go of the release. A cable release with locking screw is convenient for keeping the shutter open for prolonged periods.

Cable release: Mechanical release cable that screws into the camera's shutter release button and permits releasing without touching the camera itself. Thus reduces vibration risk with long exposure times when the camera is mounted on a tripod. A cable release with lock is more convenient.

Coma: Lens aberration that causes points of light in the subject to reproduce as elongated blurs.

Computer flash: Term sometimes applied to flash units with automatic flash duration control, i.e. where a sensor cell measures the flash light reflected from the subject and adjusts the flash duration (and hence exposure) automatically.

Old factory buildings provide a wealth of fascinating detail. With the high viewpoint the photographer could keep the camera level and avoid converging verticals.
Photo: Dr M. Beisert.

Depth of field: Zone of distances in front of the camera within which objects still appear acceptably sharp in the picture. Items at the exact distance to which the lens is set are rendered sharpest; definition gradually falls off in front of and behind that distance but this loss of definition is not apparent within the depth of field zone. A depth of field scale on each lens shows the available sharp zone at different distances and with different apertures. The sharp zone increases with smaller apertures and greater distance. Lenses of longer focal length also yield less depth of field. Sometimes confused with depth of focus, an analogous tolerance in sharpness related to the lens-to-film distance.

Electronic flash: Flash derived from a high-tension discharge between two electrodes in a tube filled with an inert gas. Yields repeatable highly intense flashes of very short duration (typically $^{1}/_{1000}$ sec) which can be further reduced — sometimes down to $^{1}/_{30\,000}$ sec — by certain types of photocell control (automatic or computer flash). Present-day compact electronic flash units fitted in the camera's flash shoe are a convenient artificial light source for photography.

Emulsion: Strictly speaking the image recording layer of film containing its light-sensitive compounds. (At certain stages of manufacture these compounds really form an emulsion-like suspension in their gelatine carrier.) More generally applied also to the film as a whole, especially when referring to its image-recording characteristics.

EV: See exposure value.

Exposure: Amount of light required to produce a developable image on the film; controlled in the camera by the lens aperture and shutter speed settings. Hence *underexposure* implies insufficient light for a picture (yields too dark slides); *overexposure* refers to too much light, producing too light slides. With negative film it is possible to compensate for some degree of under- and especially overexposure in enlarging the print. In general photographic terminology "exposure" refers to a combination of an aperture and speed setting, sometimes also simply to a picture taken in the camera.

An iris diaphragm of thin leaves controls the lens aperture by making the light-transmitting opening larger or smaller.

Exposure value (EV): Simple numerical value for the effective exposure of all equivalent aperture/speed combinations yielding the same effective exposure — e.g. $^{1}/_{15}$ sec at f/11, $^{1}/_{30}$ sec at f/8, $^{1}/_{60}$ sec at f/5.6 all yield the same effective exposure of exposure value or EV 11. Each interval of 1 EV (like an f-stop) doubles or halves the exposure. Mathematically, EV is the logarithmic sum (to base 2) of the exposure time reciprocal and of the square of the f-number, i.e. $EV = \log_2(l/t) + \log_2(\text{f-No.})^2$.

Eye relief: Optical location of viewfinder's exit pupil behind the eyepiece. With increased eye relief the eye can be further back behind the finder for comfortable viewing (e.g. when wearing glasses) — but this requires either a lower finder magnification (as in the wide-angle brilliant finders) or bulky finder optics. The eye relief of the LEICA M's finder is small — which makes the camera compact but not too convenient for viewing with glasses.

Film gate, film window: Opening inside the camera just in front of the film outlining the actual image frame. This is the real 24 × 36 mm format of the LEICA; the viewfinder shows slightly less of that image. Mounted slides also mask off some image area, as do framing masks in the negative carrier of enlargers and photofinishing printers.

Film speed: Response of senstised film to light, measured by standard procedures.

Close cropping while taking the picture often yields more impact than general views.
Photo: Dr M. Beisert.

Currently specified in ISO (International Standards Organisation) values, for instance ISO 100/21°. Here the first part (100) is an arithmetic value — double the value means double the sensitivity, requring half the exposure. The degree prt (21°) is a logarithmic speed value where speed doubles with every increase of 3°. Older LEICA M models carry film speed scales marked in ASA and/or DIN scales; these are numerically equal to the present two ISO values.

Filter factor: Indication of the exposure increase required to compensate for light absorbed by a filter. May be a numerical factor (e.g. 2×, 3×) or an exposure value correction can only be approximate — you can change the shutter speed only in whole steps and the lens aperture at best in half f-stops intervals. The pale amber or colourless filters for colour slide film usually need no correction. Filters for black-and-white film may have factors between 2× and 4× (−1 EV to −2 EV), in extreme cases up to 8×. The factor also depends on the type of film and intended effect: a higher factor (overexposure) subdues the contrast-differentiating effect of a filter on black-and-white film, underexposure (with a lower factor) enhances it. TTL metering in the LEICA M6 largely allows for the filter factor, too.

Flare: Non-image-forming scattered light within lens, reduces contrast and image quality.

Flash bulb: Flash produced by chemical combustion of aluminium or magnesium wire or foil in an oxygen atmosphere within a glass bulb. Ignited electrically to yeled an intense flash. A flash bulb is usable only once and needs a suitable flash holder for firing. Nowadays supplanted by electronic flash.

Flash socket: Synch contact at the back of a LEICA, in addition to hot shoe contact.

Flash synchronisation: Method of timing the triggering of a flash so that it lights exactly during the instant that the focal plane shutter fully uncovers the film for the exposure. Achieved by connecting the flash unit (through the hot shoe or a synch contact) to contacts built into the shutter that close at the right instant. Synchronisation with electronic falsh is only possible at slower shutter speeds where the shutter fully uncovers the film (up to 1/50 sec on the LEICA.

f-number: Numerical value of lens aperture; equal to focal length divided by the optical diameter of the lens opening (in fact the len's entrance pupil).

Focal length: Distance between a defined plane within the lens and the film plane in the camera when the lens is focused on infinity. (The reference plane can in certain cases even be located in front of or behind the lens.) The focal length determines the scale of reproduction at which a subject at a given distance is rendered on the film — the longer the focal length the larger the image. This way of image scale control is a main reason for using interchangeable lenses. On a given film format lenses of longer focal length take in a smaller angle of view than those of shorter focal length (wide-angle lenses). A 50 mm lens is regarded as the standard focal length for the 24 × 36 mm format.

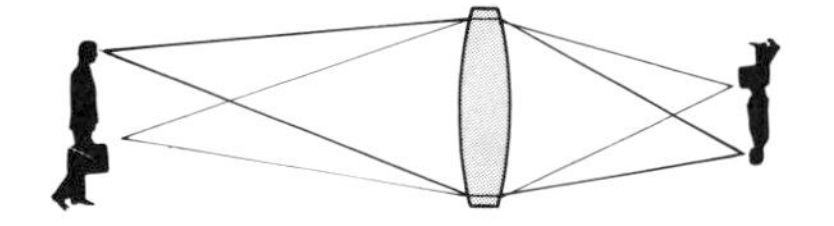

Long focal length.

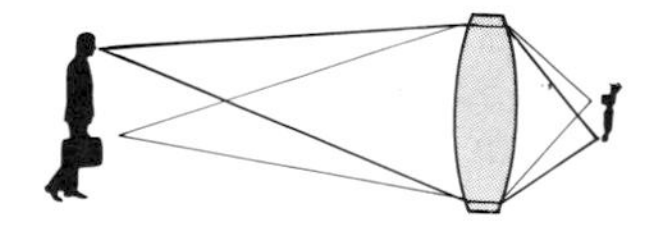

Short focal length.
A short-focus lens forms a small image close behind the lens while a longer-focus system projects the image farther back but also on a larger scale, covering on the film a smaller section of the view.

Focal plane shutter: Shutter system consisting of two blinds or curtains (fabric roller blinds in the LEICA M cameras) running past the film just in front of the camera's focal plane. The first blind uncovers the film, the second one covers it up again. With longer times (longer than 1/50 sec in the LEICA) the film is fully uncovered before the second blind starts its run. At shorter times (1/60 to 1/1000 sec) the second blind starts to close while the first is still running, in effect forming a travelling slit.

Focusing: Action of adjusting the lens-to-film distance to make the lens render objects at different distances in front of the camera sharply on the film. Usually achieved by rotating part of the lens barrel (the focusing mount) which also carries a scale to indicate the subject distance to which the lens is set. LEICA M cameras couple this movement with the built-in rangefinder.

f-stop: Generally aperture value (like f-number) but more specifically an exposure step or interval equivalent to the difference between two marked f-numbers on the aperture scale. One f-stop more exposure thus means opening the lens aperture from e.g. f/5.6 to f/4. (Same as 1 EV exposure difference i.e. a doubling or halving of the effective exposure.)

Grain: Discontinuous microstructure of the photograph image, due to the irregular distribution in the film emulsion of the crystalline light-sensitive salts. May appear disturbing in the big enlargements. Graining tends to be more prominent in high-speed films (especially black-and-white) while slower emulsions have a finer grain structure and thus can yield bigger enlargements of high quality.

Guide number: A measure of flash output, established according to international standards. With a film of ISO 100 and lens aperture f/1 is the distance (usually quoted for metres) from the subject at which the flash would yield a correctly exposed picture. In manual mode (without automatic flash duration control) the Guide No. is also an aid to working out the correct exposure. Divide the Guide No. by the flash/subject distance to get the required aperture, or by the aperture used to get the required distance. The effective Guide No. depends also on other factors (lighting angle, subject reflectivity, other reflected light etc).

Experimental portraiture. the coarse grain enhances the etching-like effect of these pictures.

Highlights: Lightest parts of the subject or image in a print or slide.

Hot shoe: Shoe on top of the LEICA to take flash units (and special viewfinders) with built-in synch contact for the flash.

Infinity: Lens setting to the shortest lens-to-film distance. A subject is reckoned to be at infinity if it is more than 2000 focal lengths away (i.e. further than 100 m with the 50 mm lens). To yield a sharp image on the film of nearer objects you have to increase the lens-to-film distance, i.e. to focus the lens.

Iris diaphragm: Set of thin metal leaves built into the lens; open or close to make the lens opening (aperture) larger or smaller for exposure control.

LED: Light-emitting diode, a minute lamp lit by comparatively small signal currents. Used in the LEICA M6 to show whether the exposure setting is correct.

Lens-hood: Front-of-lens attachment to screen the front lens surface against stray light from light sources outside the field of view. Intense light rays from such sources may be reflected from internal lens surfaces and reduce image contrast (flare); such rays may also form unwanted ghost images (usually of the lens diaphragm). Ideally, a lens hood should be used all the time for optimum image quality.

Lens speed: Largest aperture of a lens. A fast or high-speed lens has a large maximum aperture (low f-number), e.g. f/1.4, or f/1 of the NOCTILUX — one of the fastest lenses ever produced for a 35 mm camera.

Long-focus lens: Lens of longer focal length than the stndard lens; i.e. lenses from 75 mm onwards on the LEICA M. Often referred to as tele or telephoto lens, though strictly 'telephoto' implies a specific type of lens design.

Luminance: Measure of the brightness of an iluminated subject. The international unit is candelas per square metre (cd/m^2). Luminance values can compare subject brightness for exposure measurement and can specify metering limits. (Apostilb — asb — is a less used unit, 1 cd/m^2 = 3.14 asb.)

Macrophotography: Strictly, photography at a scale of reproduction larger than 1:1 (1.0×) on the film. In practice often applied to close-ups where the magnification in an average final print is likely to reach or exceed 1:1.

Background sharply focused (infinity setting) totally blurred.

Sharp focus on the foreground at full aperture kills sharpness in the distance.

By focusing halfway between the two and stopping down to a small aperture the lens extends sharpness from near to far.

Modulation transfer function (MTF): Modern measure of image quality reproduced by lenses and films. Established by measuring, often with automatic instrumentation, the contrast with which the system in question reproduces test targets at various resolution levels. By taking into account both contrast and resolution the MTF is claimed to correlate best with the visual impression of image sharpness and quality but is somewhat complex to evaluate.

Optical register: Distance from the front flange of the camera's lens mount to the film plane — 27.8 mm in the LEICA M models. All lens mounts are matched to this distance for precise operation of any LEICA M lens any LEICA M camera.

Photocell: Light-sensitive element that responds to light falling on it by generating signals in an electric circuit. These signals correspond to light intensity and may in suitable systems indicate or control the exposure required for a photographic subject. Of photocells still in use photodiodes (as used in the LEICA M6) generate or control tiny currents that are then amplified; photoresistors (e.g. in the LEICAmeter MR or in the M5) produce a signal by modifying the resistance in a circuit.

Photodiode: Type of photocell used in the LEICA M6.

Recycling time: With electronic flash units the minimum time interval between two successive flashes. Determined by the recharging delay of the power capacitors in the unit and depends on the design parameters of the unit, the current source (recycling time is often shorter with nicads) and, with modern automatic flashes, also on the flash/subject distance of the previous exposure. With near subjects only part of the flash power is used and is thus topped up much faster (sometimes within a fraction of a second).

Reproduction: see Scale.

Resolution: Mesure of the fineness of detail that an image-forming lens system and an image recording material (film) can reproduce. Usually measured by photographing or projecting targets of progressively finer black bars separated by white spaces and establishing how many such bars per unit width (line pairs per mm) can be distringuished in the image. The modern approach to image quality assessment also considers the contrast of the resulting image; that and resolution are involved in the modulation transfer function (MTF).

Scale of reproduction: Ratio in a picture of image size (of an object depicted on the film) to object size (actual size of original object). Expressed either as this ratio — e.g. a 1:5 reduction — or as a straight magnification (0.2×). In an enlarged print the scale becomes the original magnification multiplied by the degree of enlargement.

Sensor: Photocell in a flash unit, controls the flash duration in response to the amount of light reflected back from the subject. Some flash units take an external sensor mounted in the camera's flash shoe. The sensor then controls exposure reliably, even with more complex lighting set-ups.

Shadows: In exposure terms the darkest areas of a subject (and in a print or transparency) that are expected to reproduce visible tone detail.

Shutter speed: Usual reference to exposure time, i.e. period during which the shutter allows light to act on the film. Can be set on current LEICA cameras in so-called geometric steps from 1 to 1/1000 sec, with each step approximately half as long as the previous one: 1 — ½ — ¼ — ⅛ — 1/15 sec etc. A fast shutter speed implies a short time, a slow speed a long time. (At one time shutters yielded shorter times by running faster — hence 'speed'. The blinds of the LEICA shutter run at the same speed at all settings; here the interval between the blinds controls exposure times.)

Slave flash: Flash triggered by a light pulse reaching a photocell (slave cell) connected to the flash unit. That light is usually a flash mounted on, and fired by, the camera. This arrangement allows synchronised firing of any number of flash units without cumbersome synch cable connections.

Speed: See Film speed, Lens speed, Shutter speed.

Stopping down: Making the lens aperture smaller by turning the aperture ring to a higher f-number.

Synch contact: Connecting point (flash socket) for synch lead from flash units that cannot make contact through a hot shoe. (Necessary on earlier LEICAS that have no contact in the flash shoe.) Older LEICA M models have two synch contacts: one for electronic flash and one for — now hardly used — flash bulbs (the latter need different timing for the shutter contacts).

Synch time: Fastest shutter speed setting (shortest time) at which the shutter fully uncovers the film for flash synchronisation.

($^1/_{50}$ sec on LEICA M models, usually marked by a flash symbol on the shutter speed dial.)

Time exposure: Any exposure longer than the LEICA'S slowest shutter speed of 1 sec. Made by opening the shutter with a cable release at the B setting and keeping it open (by continued pressure on the release) for the required period.

Tripod bush: Threaded bush in camera baseplate, for mounting the LEICA on a tripod or table stand for a steadier support. Has a standard ¼ ″ thread.

TTL: Through the lens: usually exposure measurement by a photocell inside the camera (as in the LEICA M6 or M5), registering luminances in the image projected by the lens.

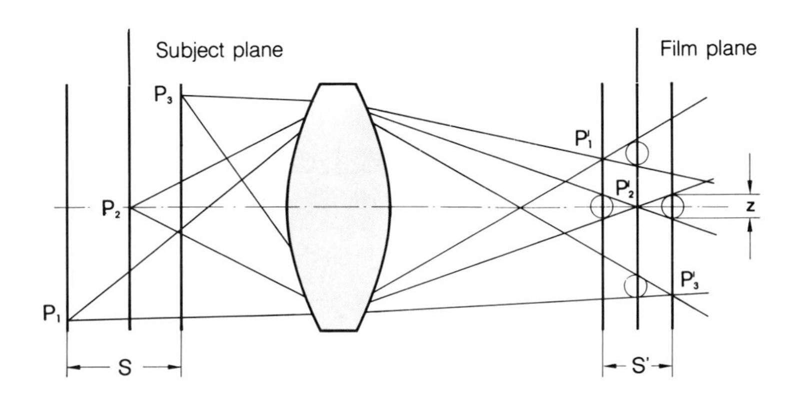

Depth of field geometry: light rays from an object point P_2 located in the exact plane on which the lens is focused forma precise image point P'_2 in the film plane. Rays from an object point —$_1$ behind the focused plane form their image point p'_1 a little in front of the image plane; in the latter that point becomes a spot of diameter z. As long as z is small enough to still appear to the eye as a point even in a bigger print, the image of objects in the plane of P_1 can be regarded as adequately sharp. The nearer object P_3 similarly projects in the film plane a small image spot of diameter z. The range S of object distances over which image spots in the film plane do not exceed a limiting size z is the depth of field.

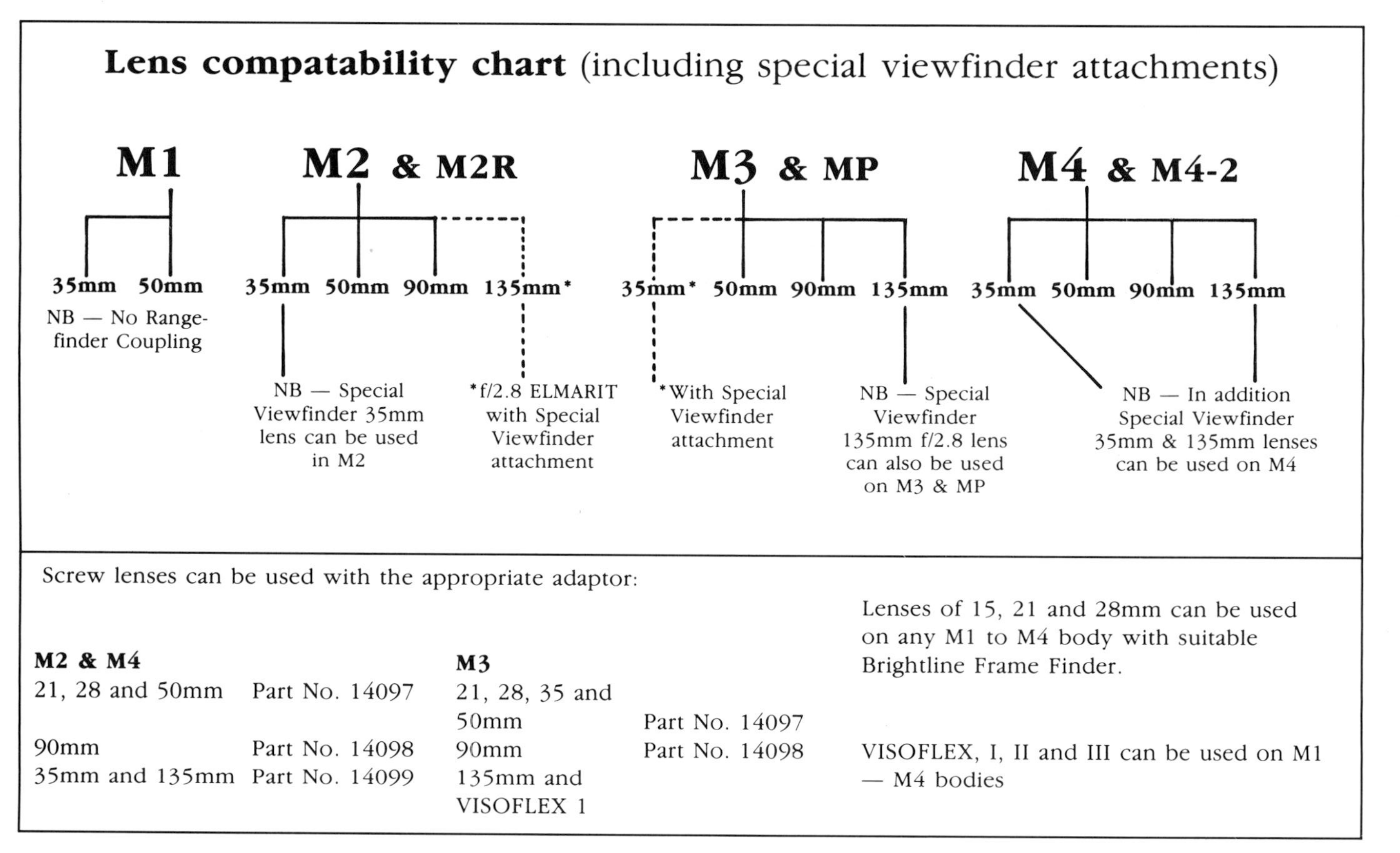
Lens compatability chart (including special viewfinder attachments)
M1
35mm 50mm
NB — No Range-finder Coupling
M2 & M2R
35mm 50mm 90mm 135mm*
NB — Special Viewfinder 35mm lens can be used in M2
*f/2.8 ELMARIT with Special Viewfinder attachment
M3 & MP
35mm* 50mm 90mm 135mm
*With Special Viewfinder attachment
NB — Special Viewfinder 135mm f/2.8 lens can also be used on M3 & MP
M4 & M4-2
35mm 50mm 90mm 135mm
NB — In addition Special Viewfinder 35mm & 135mm lenses can be used on M4
Screw lenses can be used with the appropriate adaptor:
M2 & M4
21, 28 and 50mm Part No. 14097
90mm Part No. 14098
35mm and 135mm Part No. 14099
M3
21, 28, 35 and 50mm Part No. 14097
90mm Part No. 14098
135mm and VISOFLEX 1
Lenses of 15, 21 and 28mm can be used on any M1 to M4 body with suitable Brightline Frame Finder.
VISOFLEX, I, II and III can be used on M1 — M4 bodies

Focal length & name	Max. Aperture	Min. Aperture	Angle of view Horiz.	Angle of view Diag.	Configuration Elements/groups	Near Limit ft	Near Limit m	Near Limit Scale	Dimension (mm) Length	Dimension (mm) Diam.	Filter	Weight g	Weight oz	Order Codes Lens	Order Codes Lens hood
WIDE-ANGLE AND ULTRA-WIDE ANGLE															
21 mm Elmarit-M	f/2.8	f/16	81°	92°	8/6	2.3	0.7	1:30	46.5	62	60	290	10¼	11 134	12 537 (R)
28 mm Elmarit-M	f/2.8	f/22	65°	75°	8/6	2.3	0.7	1:22	48	53	49	250	8¾	11 804	12 536 (R)
35 mm Summicron-M	f/2	f/16	54°	63°	7/5	2.3	0.7	1:18	26	52	39	150	5¼	11 310	12 524
35 mm Summilux-M	f/1.4	f/16	54°	63°	7/5	3.3	1.0	1:26	28	53	(S7)	245	8¾	11 870	12 504
STANDARD LENSES															
50 mm Summicron-M	f/2	f/16	40°	47°	6/4	2.3	0.7	1:11.5	42	52	39	195	7	11 819	12 538
50 mm Summilux-M	f/1.4	f/16	40°	47°	7/5	3.3	1.0	1:17	46	53	43	360	9¼	11 114	12 586
50 mm Noctilux	f/1	f/16	40°	47°	7/6	3.3	1.0	1:17	62	69	60	580	20½	11 821	12 539
LONGER FOCUS															
75 mm Summilux-M	f/1.4	f/16	27°	32°	7/5	3.3	1.0	1:12.5	80	68	60	625	22	11 815	built in
90 mm Tele-Elmarit-M	f/2.8	f/16	23°	27°	4/4	3.3	1.0	1:9	62	52	39	225	8	11 800	12 250 (i)
90 mm Summicron-M	f/2	f/16	23°	27°	5/4	3.3	1.0	1:9	77	63	55	460	16¼	11 136	built in
135 mm Tele-Elmar-M	f/4	f/22	15°	18°	5/3	5	1.5	1:9	105	59	39	550	19½	11 851	12 575
135 mm Elmarit-M	f/2.8	f/32	15°	18°	5/4	5	1.5	1:9	114	66	55	735	26	11 829	built in
VISOFLEX AND LONG TELE															
65 mm Elmar-V	f/3.5	f/22	31°	37°(a)	4/3	1	0.35	1:2.5(b)	55	58	44	130	4¾	11 162	built in
200 mm Telyt-V	f/4	f/22	10°	12°	4/4	10	3	1:13(c)	97(d)	72	58	640(d)	22½	11 063	built in
280 mm Telyt-V	f/4.8	f/22	7½°	9°	4/4	11½	3.5	1:10(e)	184	76	66	1200(d)	42¼	11 914	built in
400 mm Telyt-V	f/6.8	f/32	5°	6°	2/1	12	3.6	1:6.5(f)	365(h)	78	72(S7)	1830(h)	64½	11 954	built in
560 mm Telyt-V	f/6.8	f/32	3¾°	4½°	2/1	21¼	6.4	1:9(f)	510(h)	98	98(S7)	2300(h)	81	11 854	built in

General notes to table:	Dimensions (and weights) are based on manufacturer's data. The lens length is measured from the front rim to the mounting flange, with the lens set to infinity — i.e. the extent to which the lens protrudes from the camera. The diameter is the maximum diameter of the largest control ring. Filters are usually standard screw-in filters (0.5 mm pitch for 39 and 43 mm, 0.75 mm for the rest). S) are series filters (50.8 mm dia.) that fit either in the lens hood (35mm Summilux-M) or in a filter slot in the rear tube (Telyt). Lens hoods marked (R) are rectangular.
Special notes to table:	(a) With Visoflex and 16 464 helical focusing mount at shortest extension. (b) With Visoflex and 16 464 helical mount at longest extension; larger scales possible with extension tubes. (c) With appropriate adapter tube on Visofles; larger scales with extension tubes. (d) Lens in focusing mount but without Visoflex. (e) Lens on Visoflex; greater range with extension tubes. (f) With follow-focus mount, but without Visoflex. (h) Lens including follow-cocus mount, but without Visoflex. (i) Soft rubber screw-in hood; also takes 12 575 clip-on hood.

Other LEICA Titles Published by Hove Foto Books.

Modern LEICA Manuals — uniform with present volume:—

LEICA Lens Practice:	Using and Choosing LEICA Lenses by Dennis Laney
LEICA Darkroom Practice:	The Focomat Manual by Rudolf Seck

LEICA History:—

LEICA — The First 60 Years by Gianni Rogliatti
LEICA and LEICAflex Lenses, 2nd (Revised) Edition by Gianni Rogliatti

Comprehensive pocket sized guides on LEICA cameras, lenses and accessories; details of identification, dates, production, serial numbers, prices etc., for LEICA Collectors and Enthusiasts:—

LEICA Pocket Book, 3rd Edition (deals with cameras and lenses)
LEICA Accessory Guide
LEICA Price Guide

Hove Reprints:—

LEICA Catalogues for 1931, 1933, 1936, 1955, 1958, 1961, 1975.
LEICA Instruction Books for early screw, M and reflex cameras.

Write to us for full list of photo books, or in case of difficulty in obtaining any of our books. Books are available through bookshops and photo dealers or direct from the Publisher.

Hove Foto Books
34 Church Road
Hove, East Sussex
BN3 2GJ, England.